Shopify Mastery

A Comprehensive Guide to Building and Maximizing Your E-commerce Profits

Lewis Finan

Copyright 2024 by Lewis Finan - All rights reserved.

This document is geared towards providing exact and reliable information in regards to the topic and issue covered. The publication is sold with the idea that the publisher is not required to render accounting, officially permitted, or otherwise, qualified services. If advice is necessary, legal or professional, a practiced individual in the profession should be ordered.

- From a Declaration of Principles which was accepted and approved equally by a Committee of the American Bar Association and a Committee of Publishers and Associations.

In no way is it legal to reproduce, duplicate, or transmit any part of this document in either electronic means or in printed format. Recording of this publication is strictly prohibited and any storage of this document is not allowed unless with written permission from the publisher. All rights reserved.

The information provided herein is stated to be truthful and consistent, in that any liability, in terms of inattention or otherwise, by any usage or abuse of any policies, processes, or directions contained within is the solitary and utter responsibility of the recipient reader. Under no circumstances will any legal responsibility or blame be held against the publisher for any reparation, damages, or monetary loss due to the information herein, either directly or indirectly.

Respective authors own all copyrights not held by the publisher.

The information herein is offered for informational purposes solely, and is universal as so.

The presentation of the information is without contract or any type of guarantee assurance.

The trademarks that are used are without any consent, and the publication of the trademark is without permission or backing by the trademark owner. All trademarks and brands within this book are for clarifying purposes only and are the owned by the owners themselves, not affiliated with this document.

Table of Contents

Introduction 8
   Welcome to Shopify Mastery 9
   Understanding the E-commerce Landscape 11

Chapter 1: Getting Started with Shopify 16
   1.1 Setting Up Your Shopify Store 19
   1.2 Navigating the Shopify Dashboard 22
   1.3 Choosing the Right Shopify Plan for You 25

Chapter 2: Product Selection and Optimization 29
   2.1 Identifying Profitable Niches 33
   2.2 Sourcing and Selecting Winning Products 37
   2.3 Optimizing Product Pages for Conversions 42

Chapter 3: Store Design and Branding in Shopify 47
   3.1 Creating a Visually Appealing Store 52
   3.2 Building a Strong Brand Identity 53
   3.3 Enhancing User Experience on Your Shopify Store 57

Chapter 4: Marketing Strategies for E-commerce Success 62
   4.1 Crafting a Winning Marketing Plan 66
   4.2 Leveraging Social Media for Maximum Impact 71
   4.3 Implementing Effective Email Marketing Campaigns 75

Chapter 5: Maximizing Profits with Shopify 80
   5.1 Pricing Strategies for Increased Revenue 84
   5.2 Implementing Upsells and Cross-Sells: Elevating Your Sales Strategy 88
   5.3 Streamlining Your Order Fulfillment Process 90

Chapter 6: Analytics and Insights 94
   6.1 Utilizing Shopify Analytics Tools 99
   6.2 Interpreting Key E-commerce Metrics 103
   6.3 Making Data-Driven Decisions for Growth 108

Chapter 7: Scaling Your E-commerce Business 113
   7.1 Strategies for Scaling Successfully 118

7.2 Handling Increased Traffic and Orders 123

7.3 Expanding Your Product Line and Market Reach 129

Chapter 8: Troubleshooting Common Challenges 134

8.1 Overcoming Sales Plateaus 139

8.2 Dealing with Customer Service Issues 145

8.3 Staying Competitive in the E-commerce Landscape 150

Chapter 9: Future Trends in E-commerce 156

9.1 Exploring Emerging Technologies 162

9.2 Adapting to Changing Consumer Behavior 168

9.3 Positioning Your Business for Long-Term Success 174

Conclusion: 180

Introduction

Welcome to "Shopify Mastery: A Comprehensive Guide to Building and Maximizing Your E-commerce Profits." In the fast-paced world of online business, success hinges on your ability to adapt, innovate, and stay ahead of the curve. The e-commerce landscape is dynamic, and to thrive, you need more than just a product – you need a strategic approach.

Whether you're a seasoned entrepreneur or a budding e-commerce enthusiast, this book is your roadmap to mastering Shopify and unlocking the full potential of your online store. Shopify has emerged as a powerhouse in the e-commerce platform space, empowering individuals and businesses to create, manage, and scale their online presence with unprecedented ease.

In these pages, we'll delve into the intricacies of Shopify, unraveling its features and capabilities to empower you with the knowledge needed to build a successful online store. From setting up your Shopify store to implementing advanced marketing strategies, we leave no stone unturned. Our goal is not just to guide you through the technical aspects but to provide you with the insights and strategies required to stand out in a crowded digital marketplace.

Why Shopify? The answer lies in its user-friendly interface, scalability, and a plethora of tools designed to streamline the e-commerce journey. Whether you're a solo entrepreneur running a dropshipping business or a large enterprise managing an extensive product catalog, Shopify adapts to your needs, allowing you to focus on what matters – growing your business.

As we embark on this journey together, we'll cover topics such as:

1. **Setting Up Your Shopify Store**: A step-by-step guide to creating a visually appealing and user-friendly online storefront.
2. **Product Listing and Optimization**: Strategies to showcase your products effectively and optimize your listings for maximum visibility and conversions.
3. **Effective Marketing Tactics**: Dive into the world of digital marketing, including social media strategies, email campaigns, and search engine optimization, to drive traffic and boost sales.
4. **Conversion Rate Optimization (CRO)**: Learn how to turn visitors into customers by optimizing your website's design, layout, and user experience.
5. **Scaling Your Business**: Explore advanced techniques for scaling your e-commerce business, including international expansion, strategic partnerships, and inventory management.
6. **Analytics and Data-Driven Decision-Making**: Harness the power of data to make informed decisions and continually refine your strategies for optimal results.

Whether you're starting from scratch or looking to take your existing Shopify store to new heights, this guide is designed to equip you with the knowledge and tools needed to thrive in the competitive world of e-commerce. Let's embark on this journey together and unlock the full potential of your Shopify store – turning your entrepreneurial dreams into a profitable reality.

Welcome to Shopify Mastery

Welcome to "Shopify Mastery" – your gateway to unlocking the full potential of e-commerce success. In this comprehensive guide, we invite you to embark on a journey that will transform your Shopify experience, empowering you with the knowledge and strategies needed to maximize your online store's profitability.

In a world where digital entrepreneurship is on the rise, Shopify stands out as a beacon for those seeking a user-friendly and robust platform to bring their business ideas to life. This book is crafted to be your trusted companion, offering insights, tips, and practical advice to not only navigate the intricacies of Shopify but also to elevate your e-commerce venture to new heights.

As we delve into the core aspects of Shopify Mastery, you can expect to:

- **Navigate the Shopify Ecosystem**: We'll guide you through the process of setting up your Shopify store, ensuring a seamless and efficient start to your online business journey.
- **Optimize Your Product Presence**: Learn the art of creating compelling product listings, optimizing them for search engines, and capturing the attention of your target audience.
- **Master Marketing Strategies**: From social media tactics to email campaigns, we'll unravel the secrets of effective digital marketing, helping you drive traffic, engage customers, and boost sales.
- **Enhance Conversion Rates**: Explore the principles of Conversion Rate Optimization (CRO) to turn website visitors into loyal customers, maximizing the impact of your online presence.
- **Scale Your Business**: Whether you're a solo entrepreneur or managing a growing enterprise, discover proven techniques to scale

your Shopify business successfully, both nationally and internationally.
- **Harness Analytics for Success**: Dive into the world of data-driven decision-making, utilizing analytics to refine your strategies, identify opportunities, and stay ahead of market trends.

"Shopify Mastery" is not just a guide – it's a roadmap to navigate the dynamic e-commerce landscape and build a thriving online business. Whether you're just starting or looking to enhance your existing store, the knowledge contained within these pages will empower you to transform your Shopify store into a profitable venture.

Get ready to turn your aspirations into reality and embark on a journey that will redefine your e-commerce success. Welcome to "Shopify Mastery" – where your entrepreneurial dreams meet strategic excellence.

Understanding the E-commerce Landscape

E-commerce, short for electronic commerce, has evolved into a transformative force, reshaping the way businesses operate and consumers shop. This digital revolution has not only changed the retail sector but has become a fundamental aspect of global commerce. To navigate the vast and dynamic e-commerce landscape, it's essential to grasp the key elements that define this ever-evolving ecosystem.

1. **Digital Storefronts:**

The traditional brick-and-mortar store has found its virtual counterpart in digital storefronts. E-commerce enables businesses to showcase and sell their products or services online, offering customers the convenience of browsing, selecting, and purchasing from the comfort of their homes.

2. Diverse Business Models:

E-commerce accommodates a multitude of business models, from traditional retail models to innovative concepts like dropshipping, subscription services, and digital product sales. Each model caters to different market needs and consumer preferences.

3. Ecosystem Platforms:

E-commerce platforms, such as Shopify, WooCommerce, and Magento, provide the infrastructure for businesses to build and manage their online presence. These platforms offer customizable solutions, enabling entrepreneurs to create unique digital storefronts without extensive technical expertise.

4. Payment Gateways:

Secure and efficient payment processing is integral to e-commerce. Payment gateways like PayPal, Stripe, and Square facilitate online transactions, ensuring a seamless and trustworthy buying experience for customers.

5. Logistics and Fulfillment:

Efficient supply chain management and logistics play a crucial role in the success of e-commerce. From order fulfillment to shipping and delivery, businesses must strategize to meet customer expectations regarding speed, cost, and reliability.

6. Digital Marketing Strategies:

E-commerce success hinges on effective digital marketing. Strategies such as search engine optimization (SEO), social media marketing, email campaigns, and influencer collaborations help businesses reach their target audience, drive traffic, and boost sales.

7. Mobile Commerce (M-commerce):

With the proliferation of smartphones, mobile commerce has become a significant component of e-commerce. Responsive websites and dedicated mobile apps allow businesses to tap into the growing number of consumers who prefer shopping on their mobile devices.

8. Data Analytics and Personalization:

Data-driven decision-making is a hallmark of successful e-commerce. Analyzing customer behavior, preferences, and trends enables businesses to tailor their offerings and marketing strategies, creating personalized and engaging experiences for consumers.

9. Global Reach:

E-commerce transcends geographical boundaries, offering businesses the opportunity to reach a global audience. Cross-border trade has become more accessible, allowing businesses of all sizes to expand their markets internationally.

As we navigate the e-commerce landscape, it's crucial to adapt to emerging trends, technological advancements, and shifting consumer behaviors. The ability to understand and leverage these elements will empower businesses to thrive in the dynamic and competitive world of e-commerce.

Chapter 1: Getting Started with Shopify

In the ever-expanding realm of e-commerce, setting up a strong foundation is key to the success of your online venture. Shopify, with its user-friendly interface and robust features, stands out as an ideal platform for creating and managing your online store. In this chapter, we will guide you through the essential steps to get started with Shopify, from creating your account to setting up your first storefront.

1. Creating Your Shopify Account:

The first step on your Shopify journey is creating an account. Navigate to the Shopify website and sign up by providing the necessary information. Once registered, you'll gain access to the Shopify dashboard – the central hub for managing your store.

2. Choosing Your Store Name and URL:

Your store's name and URL are crucial components of your brand identity. Select a name that reflects your business and resonates with your target audience. Shopify allows you to check the availability of your chosen domain name and provides suggestions if needed.

3. Setting Up Your Store:

With your account and domain secured, it's time to set up your store. Shopify's intuitive setup wizard will guide you through the process, prompting you to enter key details such as your business address, currency preferences, and product types. Take the time to configure these settings to align with your business goals.

4. Choosing a Shopify Plan:

Shopify offers various pricing plans tailored to different business needs. Evaluate your requirements and choose a plan that aligns with your budget and growth expectations. Each plan comes with its own set of features, such as advanced analytics, gift cards, and lower transaction fees.

5. Customizing Your Store's Look and Feel:

Make your store visually appealing and unique by customizing its appearance. Shopify provides a range of customizable themes to choose from. Select a theme that complements your brand, and use the theme editor to adjust colors, fonts, and layout to suit your preferences.

6. Adding Your Products:

The heart of your Shopify store lies in the products you offer. Learn how to add and manage your products effectively. This includes uploading high-quality images, writing compelling product descriptions, and organizing your inventory for a seamless shopping experience.

7. Setting Up Payment Gateways:

Secure and efficient payment processing is critical for online transactions. Shopify integrates with various payment gateways, including PayPal, Stripe, and credit card processors. Configure your preferred payment methods to ensure a smooth checkout process for your customers.

8. Launching Your Store:

Congratulations, you're almost ready to launch! Before making your store live, conduct thorough testing to ensure all functionalities work as intended. Check your checkout process, test payment methods, and review your store's overall user experience. Once satisfied, hit the launch button and introduce your brand to the online world.

As you embark on your Shopify journey, remember that this chapter is just the beginning. The subsequent chapters will delve into more advanced features, strategies, and techniques to help you not only manage but thrive in the competitive landscape of e-commerce. Welcome to the world of Shopify – where your online business dreams begin to take shape.

1.1 Setting Up Your Shopify Store

Congratulations on choosing Shopify as your e-commerce platform! In this section, we will guide you through the initial steps of setting up your Shopify store, ensuring a smooth and efficient process from the very beginning.

Step 1: Create Your Shopify Account

Visit the Shopify website and click on the "Get Started" button. Follow the prompts to create your account by entering your email, password, and store name. Take your time to select a unique and memorable store name as it will become an integral part of your brand identity.

Step 2: Enter Your Store Details

Once your account is created, you'll be directed to the Shopify dashboard. Start by entering essential details about your store, including your business address and contact information. This information is crucial for order fulfillment and customer communication.

Step 3: Choose Your Store's URL

Selecting a distinctive and easily memorable URL (web address) is a key part of your brand identity. Shopify allows you to check the availability of your chosen domain name and provides alternatives if needed. Take your time in choosing a URL that aligns with your brand and is easy for customers to remember.

Step 4: Configure Your Store Settings

Navigate to the "Settings" tab on the dashboard and configure your store settings. This includes selecting your currency, time zone, and preferred units of measurement. These settings ensure that your store operates seamlessly and accurately reflects your business context.

Step 5: Choose a Shopify Plan

Shopify offers various pricing plans to cater to different business needs. Review the features and limitations of each plan, then choose the one that aligns with your budget and growth expectations. You can always upgrade your plan as your business expands.

Step 6: Customize Your Store's Look and Feel

Make your store visually appealing and unique by customizing its appearance. Shopify provides a selection of themes that you can customize to match your brand. Use the theme editor to adjust colors, fonts, and layout, creating a cohesive and attractive storefront.

Step 7: Add Your First Products

The heart of your Shopify store lies in the products you offer. Navigate to the "Products" tab and start adding your first products. Include high-quality images, detailed descriptions, and accurate inventory information to provide customers with a comprehensive view of your offerings.

Step 8: Set Up Payment Gateways

Secure and efficient payment processing is crucial for a successful online store. Configure your preferred payment gateways, such as PayPal, Stripe, or credit card processors, to provide customers with diverse and trustworthy payment options.

Step 9: Test Your Store

Before making your store live, conduct thorough testing. Go through the checkout process, test payment methods, and ensure all functionalities work seamlessly. This step is crucial to providing a positive experience for your customers from the moment your store goes live.

Congratulations, you've completed the initial setup of your Shopify store! This foundation will serve as the launching pad for your e-commerce journey. In the upcoming sections, we will delve into more advanced features and strategies to help you optimize and grow your online business. Welcome to the world of Shopify!

1.2 Navigating the Shopify Dashboard

Welcome to the command center of your e-commerce venture – the Shopify Dashboard. This central hub is where you'll manage and monitor every aspect of your online store. In this section, we'll guide you through the key elements of the Shopify Dashboard, empowering you to navigate with confidence.

1. Overview of the Dashboard:

Upon logging in, you'll land on the Dashboard, presenting a snapshot of your store's recent activities, including sales, orders, and visitor traffic. Familiarize yourself with this overview as it provides a quick insight into your store's performance.

2. Left Sidebar Menu:

The left sidebar houses the main navigation menu, categorizing key functionalities. Let's explore some crucial sections:

- **Orders**: Track and manage customer orders, process payments, and handle fulfillment.
- **Products**: Add, edit, and organize your product listings, including images, descriptions, and pricing.
- **Customers**: Manage customer information, track their orders, and analyze their purchasing behavior.

- **Analytics**: Dive into detailed reports on sales, customer behavior, and traffic to make informed decisions.
- **Marketing**: Access tools for creating discounts, launching campaigns, and managing your online presence.
- **Online Store**: Customize your store's appearance, manage themes, and configure essential settings.
- **Apps**: Explore and install Shopify apps to enhance your store's functionality and performance.

3. Notification Center:

Located at the top-right corner, the notification center alerts you to important updates, orders, and other critical information. Stay vigilant to promptly address any action items.

4. Sales Overview:

Directly beneath the Dashboard, you'll find a breakdown of your store's sales performance. Monitor sales trends, track your best-selling products, and identify areas for improvement.

5. Quick Access to Key Tasks:

The central area of the Dashboard provides quick links to essential tasks. Create a new product, view recent activity, or navigate to critical sections with just a click.

6. Online Store Customization:

Under the "Online Store" section, explore the "Themes" and "Customize" options. Here, you can personalize your store's appearance, modify themes, and tailor the layout to match your brand identity.

7. Reports and Analytics:

Utilize the "Analytics" section for in-depth insights into your store's performance. Analyze sales trends, understand customer behavior, and make data-driven decisions to optimize your strategy.

8. App Integration:

Visit the "Apps" section to explore the Shopify App Store. Integrate apps to enhance functionalities, from marketing tools to customer support and inventory management.

Navigating the Shopify Dashboard is a foundational skill for effective store management. As you delve into each section, you'll gain a deeper understanding of your store's dynamics and uncover growth opportunities. In the subsequent chapters, we'll explore specific aspects of the Dashboard in greater detail, ensuring you make the most of Shopify's powerful features. Happy navigating!

1.3 Choosing the Right Shopify Plan for You

Selecting the appropriate Shopify plan is a pivotal decision that shapes the foundation of your e-commerce journey. Shopify offers a range of plans tailored to different business needs, each with its own set of features and pricing. In this section, we'll guide you through the factors to consider when choosing the right Shopify plan for your unique requirements.

1. Basic Shopify:

- Ideal for small businesses or those just starting in the e-commerce space.
- Cost-effective with essential features to set up and manage your online store.
- Suitable for businesses with a modest product catalog and moderate sales volume.
- Transaction fees apply for payments processed outside of Shopify Payments.

2. Shopify:

- A balanced plan catering to growing businesses with expanding needs.
- Offers additional features like professional reports and abandoned cart recovery.

- Suitable for businesses with a growing product range and increasing sales volume.
- Lower transaction fees compared to Basic Shopify for external payment gateways.

3. Advanced Shopify:

- Geared towards established businesses with significant sales volumes.
- Includes advanced reporting tools and third-party calculated shipping rates.
- Ideal for businesses with a broad product range and high transaction volumes.
- Lowest transaction fees for external payment gateways among the Shopify plans.

4. Shopify Plus:

- An enterprise-level solution for high-volume businesses with complex requirements.
- Customizable and scalable to accommodate large product catalogs and extensive sales.
- Offers advanced features, dedicated support, and tailor-made solutions.
- Custom pricing based on individual business needs.

Factors to Consider:

- **Budget:**

Evaluate your budgetary constraints and choose a plan that aligns with your financial resources. Consider not just the current costs but also potential future expenses as your business expands.

- **Business Growth:**

Select a plan that accommodates your anticipated business growth. A scalable plan ensures that your e-commerce platform evolves with your expanding product range, customer base, and sales volume.

- **Feature Requirements:**

Identify the features essential for your business operations. Consider factors such as advanced reporting, abandoned cart recovery, and third-party calculated shipping rates to determine which plan aligns with your feature requirements.

- **Transaction Fees:**

Be aware of transaction fees associated with each plan, especially if you plan to use external payment gateways. Understanding these fees will help you calculate the overall cost of using Shopify for your transactions.

- **Support and Resources:**

Evaluate the level of support and additional resources offered with each plan. Advanced plans often provide priority support and access to exclusive features that can be beneficial for businesses requiring extra assistance.

- **Shopify Plus Consideration:**

If you operate a large enterprise with complex needs, explore the capabilities of Shopify Plus. While it comes with a custom price tag, it offers a suite of advanced features and dedicated support tailored to enterprise-level businesses.

Choosing the right Shopify plan is a strategic decision that directly influences your store's capabilities and growth potential. Assess your business needs comprehensively, and select a plan that not only meets your current requirements but also aligns with your future ambitions in the dynamic world of e-commerce.

Chapter 2: Product Selection and Optimization

In the vast landscape of e-commerce, the success of your online store hinges on the careful curation and presentation of your products. Chapter 2 focuses on the pivotal elements of product selection and optimization, guiding you through the process of building a compelling product lineup and ensuring each item maximizes its potential within your Shopify store.

1. Crafting a Winning Product Selection Strategy:

- Understand Your Target Audience: Identify the preferences, needs, and pain points of your target customers to curate a product selection that resonates with them.

- Market Research: Analyze market trends, competitor offerings, and customer reviews to discover gaps in the market and opportunities for differentiation.

2. Adding Products to Your Shopify Store:

- Product Listings: Create detailed and visually appealing product listings that showcase your items effectively.
- High-Quality Imagery: Invest in professional-quality product images to provide customers with a clear and enticing view of your offerings.
- Compelling Descriptions: Craft engaging and informative product descriptions that highlight key features and benefits.

3. Organizing Your Product Catalog:

- Categories and Collections: Organize your products into logical categories and collections to facilitate easy navigation for your customers.
- Tags and Filters: Implement tags and filters to enhance the searchability of your products, allowing customers to find what they need quickly.

4. Product Pricing Strategies:

- Cost Analysis: Conduct a thorough cost analysis, considering production, shipping, and operational expenses, to determine appropriate pricing.
- Competitive Pricing: Research competitor pricing to ensure your products remain competitive in the market.

5. Inventory Management:

- Stock Levels: Keep a close eye on stock levels to prevent overselling and ensure a positive customer experience.
- Backorders and Pre-orders: Implement backorder and pre-order options when applicable to manage customer expectations during high-demand periods.

6. Optimizing for Search Engines (SEO):

- Keyword Research: Identify relevant keywords related to your products to optimize product titles, descriptions, and Meta tags for search engines.
- Product URLs: Create clean and concise URLs for each product to enhance search engine visibility.

7. Utilizing Shopify Apps for Product Enhancement:

Explore Shopify's App Store for apps that can enhance your product pages, such as reviews and ratings, product recommendations, and advanced search functionalities.

8. Implementing Cross-selling and Up-selling Strategies:

- Cross-selling: Encourage customers to add complementary items to their cart during the checkout process.
- Up-selling: Suggest higher-tier or premium versions of products to boost average order value.

9. Monitoring Product Performance:

- Shopify Analytics: Leverage Shopify's analytics tools to track the performance of each product, identifying top sellers and areas for improvement.
- Customer Feedback: Pay attention to customer reviews and feedback to understand their experiences with your products and make necessary adjustments.

Chapter 2 equips you with the knowledge and strategies to curate a winning product lineup and optimize each item for maximum impact. As we delve deeper into the intricacies of product management, you'll gain valuable insights into refining your product selection and creating a shopping experience that captivates your audience. Let's elevate your product game and set the stage for a thriving online store.

2.1 Identifying Profitable Niches

In the ever-expanding world of e-commerce, the key to success lies in finding and capitalizing on profitable niches. A niche market allows you to focus your efforts on a specific segment of the population with distinct needs and preferences. This section delves into the strategies and considerations for identifying profitable niches that align with your business goals.

Understanding Niches:

Definition: A niche is a specialized segment of the market for a particular kind of product or service. It involves targeting a specific audience with unique needs that may be underserved by broader markets.

Benefits of Niche Marketing:

- Reduced Competition: Focusing on a niche can help you stand out in a less saturated market.
- Targeted Marketing: Tailor your marketing efforts to a specific audience, increasing the relevance of your messaging.

- Customer Loyalty: Serving a niche allows you to build strong relationships with customers who value your specialized offerings.

Strategies for Identifying Profitable Niches:

1. **Personal Passion and Expertise:**

Consider your interests, hobbies, and expertise. Identifying a niche aligned with your passions can lead to a more fulfilling and sustainable business.

2. **Market Research:**

Conduct thorough market research to identify gaps and opportunities. Analyze competitors, customer reviews, and industry trends to uncover areas with untapped potential.

3. **Target Audience Analysis:**

Understand the demographics, preferences, and pain points of your target audience. A deep understanding of your potential customers helps tailor your niche to their specific needs.

4. **Trend Analysis:**

Stay informed about current and emerging trends. Assess whether a trend has the potential to evolve into a long-term niche market or if it presents a short-lived opportunity.

5. **Problem Solving:**

Identify problems or challenges within a specific market segment and offer solutions through your products or services. A niche that addresses genuine needs can attract a dedicated customer base.

6. **Keyword Research:**

Utilize keyword research tools to identify search terms related to potential niches. High search volumes with moderate competition may indicate a lucrative niche.

7. **Analyzing Profitability:**

Evaluate the potential profitability of a niche by considering factors such as production costs, pricing flexibility, and the willingness of customers to pay for specialized products.

8. **Niche Validation:**

Test the viability of a niche with a small-scale launch or a pilot program. Monitor customer response and adjust your approach based on the feedback received.

9. Industry Partnerships:

Explore partnerships with other businesses or influencers within a niche. Collaborations can provide valuable insights and expand your reach within a specific market.

10. Evergreen Niches:

Consider evergreen niches that have consistent demand over time. These niches may not be as susceptible to seasonal fluctuations.

Case Studies and Success Stories:

Examine case studies and success stories within your industry or related niches. Learn from others who have successfully identified and capitalized on profitable niche markets.

Identifying profitable niches is a strategic process that requires a combination of creativity, research, and a keen understanding of market dynamics. By honing in on niches that align with your expertise and resonate with your target audience, you can position your e-commerce business for sustained growth and success.

2.2 Sourcing and Selecting Winning Products

The success of your e-commerce venture is intricately tied to the products you offer. Selecting winning products involves a strategic approach to sourcing items that not only align with market demand but also resonate with your target audience. This section explores the essential steps and considerations for sourcing and selecting products that can elevate your online store.

Understanding Your Target Audience:

- Demographics and Preferences: Develop a deep understanding of your target audience's demographics, preferences, and buying behavior.
- Market Research: Conduct market research to identify trends, gaps, and opportunities within your niche.

Sourcing Strategies:

1. Manufacturer and Supplier Research:

Identify reputable manufacturers or suppliers that align with your product quality standards.

Evaluate their production capacity, lead times, and reliability.

2. Quality Control:

Implement stringent quality control measures to ensure the products meet or exceed customer expectations.

Request product samples and assess them for quality before committing to bulk orders.

3. Cost Analysis:

Perform comprehensive cost analysis, considering manufacturing or wholesale costs, shipping fees, and potential tariffs or duties.

Determine a pricing strategy that allows for a profitable margin while remaining competitive.

4. Trend Analysis:

Stay informed about industry trends and consumer preferences.

Balance trendy products with evergreen items to maintain a diverse product range.

5. Seasonal Considerations:

Anticipate seasonal demands and adjust your product selection accordingly.

Plan for inventory management to prevent overstocking or shortages during peak seasons.

6. Unique Value Proposition (UVP):

Identify what makes your products unique in the market.

Emphasize your Unique Value Proposition (UVP) in marketing materials to differentiate your offerings.

7. Sustainability and Ethical Sourcing:

Consider sourcing products that align with sustainability and ethical standards.

Highlight eco-friendly practices or fair trade aspects to appeal to conscious consumers.

Product Selection Criteria:

1. Demand and Market Trends:

Choose products with demonstrated demand in the market.

Monitor trends and adapt your product selection to align with consumer preferences.

2. Profitability Potential:

Assess the potential profitability of each product, factoring in costs and market pricing.

Focus on products with a healthy profit margin.

3. Scalability:

Evaluate the scalability of your product selection.

Choose items that can be easily scaled to meet growing demand without compromising quality.

4. Complementary Products:

Offer complementary products that encourage upselling and cross-selling.

Create bundled packages to increase the average order value.

5. Brand Cohesiveness:

Ensure your product selection aligns with your brand identity and target audience.

Maintain a cohesive aesthetic across all products to strengthen brand recognition.

6. Customer Feedback:

Consider customer feedback and reviews when selecting and curating your product lineup.

Use feedback to make informed decisions on product improvements or discontinuations.

Testing and Iteration:

Test new products with a limited release or through a pilot program.

Monitor customer response and iterate your product selection based on performance.

Selecting winning products is an ongoing process that requires a combination of strategic planning, market analysis, and a keen understanding of your target audience. By aligning your product selection with market demand and your brand values, you can create a curated lineup that resonates with customers and positions your e-commerce store for success.

2.3 Optimizing Product Pages for Conversions

Your product pages serve as the digital storefront of your online business, making the optimization of these pages critical for maximizing conversions. In this section, we'll delve into strategies and best practices to ensure your product pages are not only visually appealing but also designed to guide visitors seamlessly through the buying process.

1. **Compelling Product Descriptions:**

Craft clear, compelling, and concise product descriptions that highlight key features and benefits.

Use persuasive language to convey the unique selling points of each product.

Ensure readability by breaking down information into bullet points and short paragraphs.

2. **High-Quality Product Images:**

Feature high-resolution images that showcase the product from multiple angles.

Include zoom-in functionality for customers to examine product details.

Utilize lifestyle images to help customers visualize product use.

3. Clear and Prominent Call-to-Action (CTA):

Place a clear and prominent "Add to Cart" or "Buy Now" button above the fold.

Use contrasting colors for CTA buttons to make them stand out.

Create a sense of urgency with compelling CTAs, such as "Limited Stock" or "Special Offer."

4. Detailed Product Specifications:

Provide detailed product specifications, including dimensions, materials, and any relevant technical details.

Answer potential customer questions by preemptively addressing common concerns in the product specifications.

5. Customer Reviews and Ratings:

Display customer reviews and ratings prominently on the product page.

Encourage satisfied customers to leave positive reviews, enhancing social proof.

Respond to customer reviews, showing engagement and commitment to customer satisfaction.

6. **Mobile Optimization:**

Ensure that product pages are optimized for mobile devices to accommodate the growing number of mobile shoppers.

Test the user experience on various devices to guarantee seamless navigation.

7. **Pricing Transparency:**

Display the product price, including any discounts or promotions.

Offer transparent information about shipping costs and any additional fees.

Use tiered pricing or package deals to encourage higher-value purchases.

8. **Trust Badges and Security Assurance:**

Display trust badges and security seals to instill confidence in customers.

Assure customers of secure payment processing and data protection.

Highlight any industry certifications or guarantees.

9. **Cross-Selling and Up-Selling:**

Implement cross-selling and up-selling strategies by suggesting related products or premium versions.

Showcase bundled deals or product combinations to increase the average order value.

10. **User-Friendly Navigation:**

Ensure easy navigation with a well-organized layout.

Implement intuitive and user-friendly menus for quick access to product categories.

Use breadcrumbs to help customers understand their position within the site structure.

11. **Live Chat and Customer Support:**

Offer live chat or easy access to customer support for real-time assistance.

Address customer queries promptly to enhance trust and encourage conversions.

12. **Clear Return and Refund Policies:**

Communicate return and refund policies on the product page.

Assure a hassle-free return process, fostering customer confidence.

13. Social Media Integration:

Include social media sharing buttons to encourage customers to share their favorite products.

Display Instagram or user-generated content to showcase products in real-life scenarios.

14. A/B Testing:

Conduct A/B testing on various elements, such as CTA buttons, images, or product descriptions.

Analyze the data to optimize for the elements that contribute to higher conversions.

By implementing these optimization strategies, you can transform your product pages into conversion-centric assets that not only showcase your products effectively but also guide visitors toward making confident purchasing decisions. Regularly analyze performance metrics and adapt your approach to continually enhance the conversion potential of your product pages.

Chapter 3: Store Design and Branding in Shopify

In the realm of e-commerce, the visual appeal and branding of your Shopify store are instrumental in creating a memorable and immersive shopping experience. This chapter delves into the intricacies of store design and branding specific to Shopify, guiding you through the process of crafting a distinct online presence that captivates visitors and fosters brand loyalty.

1. **Crafting a Distinctive Brand Identity:**

- Shopify Theme Selection: Explore Shopify's extensive theme library to find a design that aligns with your brand identity.
- Customization: Tailor your chosen theme to reflect your brand's color scheme, typography, and overall aesthetic.
- Logo Integration: Ensure seamless integration of your logo within the theme for consistent branding.

2. **Customizing Your Shopify Logo:**

- Logo Placement: Strategically place your logo in the header for maximum visibility.
- File Optimization: Upload a high-resolution version of your logo to maintain clarity across different screen sizes.
- Mobile Responsiveness: Confirm that your logo scales appropriately for a cohesive mobile experience.

3. **Consistent Visual Branding:**

- Theme Color Customization: Utilize Shopify's theme customization options to match your color palette.
- Typography Control: Adjust font styles and sizes within the theme settings for a consistent typography approach.
- Imagery Guidelines: Establish guidelines for product images, ensuring a uniform style that aligns with your brand.

4. **User-Friendly and Intuitive Navigation:**

   - Menu Customization: Customize your navigation menu to reflect your product categories or collections.
   - Mega Menus: Implement mega menus for larger stores with extensive product offerings.
   - Search Bar Optimization: Ensure an easily accessible and prominent search bar for seamless navigation.

5. **Engaging Homepage Design:**

   - Section Customization: Leverage Shopify's section customization to design an engaging homepage.
   - Featured Products: Showcase featured products or collections in visually appealing sections.
   - Promotional Banners: Integrate promotional banners for highlighting special offers or announcements.

6. **Building Trust with Trust Signals:**

   - Trust Badge Integration: Display trust badges at key touchpoints, such as the checkout and product pages.

- Customer Testimonials Section: Create a dedicated section for customer testimonials on your homepage.
- Contact Information Visibility: Ensure clear visibility of contact information, building trust through accessibility.

7. **Checkout Process Optimization:**

- Shopify Checkout Customization: Customize the Shopify checkout settings to streamline the process.
- Guest Checkout Promotion: Promote the convenience of guest checkout during the purchasing journey.
- Shipping Policy Transparency: Communicate shipping policies and costs at checkout.

8. **Creating a Blog or Content Section:**

- Shopify Blog Integration: Integrate Shopify's built-in blogging platform for content creation.
- SEO Optimization: Optimize blog content for SEO to enhance your store's visibility.
- Brand Storytelling: Leverage the blog to narrate your brand story and connect with your audience.

9. **Social Media Integration:**

- Social Sharing Buttons: Enable social sharing buttons on product pages to encourage customer engagement.
- Instagram Feed Integration: Utilize Shopify apps to seamlessly integrate your Instagram feed into your store.
- Consistent Branding across Platforms: Maintain a cohesive brand voice and visuals on all social media platforms.

10. **Regular Brand Audits and Adaptations:**

- Shopify Analytics Utilization: Leverage Shopify Analytics to gain insights into visitor behavior and preferences.
- Adaptation to Growth: As your Shopify store grows, revisit your branding to align with evolving goals and offerings.
- Competitor Analysis within Shopify Ecosystem: Explore other successful Shopify stores for inspiration and strategic insights.

By harnessing the features and flexibility offered by Shopify, you can design a visually stunning and brand-consistent online store. This chapter serves as a guide to navigating Shopify's design and branding tools, empowering you to create a compelling storefront that not only attracts customers but also leaves a lasting impression. As we progress, we'll explore additional strategies to optimize your Shopify store for success in the competitive e-commerce landscape.

3.1 Creating a Visually Appealing Store

Creating a visually appealing Shopify store is a critical endeavor in establishing a strong online presence and enticing customers to engage with your brand. Begin by carefully selecting a theme from Shopify's diverse collection, ensuring it aligns seamlessly with your brand's identity. Choose a theme that not only complements your color palette and aesthetics but also provides a responsive design for a consistent experience across various devices. Strategically place your logo in a prominent position, utilizing consistent typography and a cohesive color scheme to reinforce brand recognition.

Invest in high-quality product imagery, capturing your offerings from multiple angles and incorporating lifestyle shots to enhance the visual narrative. Maintain a uniform style for all images to create a polished and cohesive look throughout your store. Design an intuitive navigation menu, promoting easy exploration of product categories and other essential sections. Embrace whitespace strategically to avoid visual clutter, allowing visitors to focus on key elements. Consider grid layouts for product listings to ensure a clean and organized presentation.

Enhance your homepage with captivating elements, such as a dynamic hero banner, featured product showcases, and promotional banners for ongoing offers or new arrivals. Implement interactive features like product zoom functionality and slider carousels to add dynamism. Position clear and compelling calls-to-action (CTAs) strategically throughout your store, using contrasting colors and persuasive copy to guide visitors toward desired actions.

Prioritize mobile-friendly design to cater to the growing number of users accessing your store via smartphones and tablets. Ensure a responsive layout and optimize the user experience for touch interactions and smaller screens. Incorporate trust-building elements such as trust badges, snippets of customer testimonials, and clear communication of policies to instill confidence in potential buyers.

Integrate social media seamlessly into your Shopify store by including social links and embedding an Instagram feed to showcase your brand's visual appeal. Leverage user-generated content to turn satisfied customers into brand advocates. Regularly update your store with seasonal refreshes, ensuring banners, product highlights, and color schemes align with current trends or promotional events. Conduct routine maintenance checks to address broken links and optimize performance, contributing to a seamless and enjoyable shopping experience for your customers. Through a thoughtful and detailed approach, your visually appealing Shopify store becomes a powerful tool for establishing a strong brand presence and driving customer engagement.

3.2 Building a Strong Brand Identity

In the ever-evolving landscape of e-commerce, building a robust brand identity is the cornerstone of creating a memorable and recognizable presence. Your brand identity encompasses the essence of your business, shaping how customers perceive and connect with your products or services. This section outlines key strategies to craft a strong and distinctive brand identity that resonates with your target audience and sets your online store apart in the competitive marketplace.

1. **Define Your Brand Mission and Values:**

Clearly articulate your brand's mission, outlining the purpose and impact you aim to achieve.

Establish core values that reflect the principles and beliefs driving your business.

2. **Develop a Unique Brand Personality:**

Determine the personality traits that define your brand, influencing communication style, visuals, and overall tone.

Consider whether your brand is playful, sophisticated, innovative, or authoritative.

3. **Align with Your Target Audience:**

Understand the demographics, preferences, and aspirations of your target audience.

Tailor your brand identity to resonate with the values and lifestyle of your ideal customers.

4. Consistent Visual Branding:

Design a memorable logo that encapsulates your brand's essence and is easily recognizable.

Establish a cohesive color palette and use consistent typography across all brand assets.

5. Craft a Unique Selling Proposition (USP):

Identify what sets your brand apart from competitors.

Communicate a clear and compelling Unique Selling Proposition that addresses customer needs.

6. Brand Storytelling:

Develop a narrative that narrates the journey of your brand, its origins, and the values it stands for.

Use storytelling across your website, social media, and marketing materials to create an emotional connection with customers.

7. Establish Brand Guidelines:

Create comprehensive brand guidelines outlining the proper usage of logos, colors, fonts, and other visual elements.

Ensure consistency in brand representation across all channels.

8. Build Brand Recognition:

Consistently apply your brand elements, such as logos and colors, across your website, packaging, and marketing materials.

Engage in brand-building activities, such as collaborations, sponsorships, or influencer partnerships.

9. Foster Community Engagement:

Cultivate a sense of community around your brand through social media engagement, forums, or user-generated content.

Encourage customers to share their experiences and connect with your brand on a personal level.

10. Adaptability for Growth:

Design a brand identity that allows for evolution and adaptation as your business grows.

Anticipate changes in the market and consumer trends, ensuring your brand remains relevant.

11. Monitor and Iterate:

Regularly assess the performance of your brand identity through customer feedback, analytics, and market trends.

Be open to refining elements of your brand identity to better align with customer expectations and industry shifts.

Building a strong brand identity is an ongoing process that requires a deep understanding of your business values, target audience, and the competitive landscape. By incorporating these strategies, you can establish a brand that not only stands out but also resonates authentically with customers, fostering loyalty and trust in the long run.

3.3 Enhancing User Experience on Your Shopify Store

In the dynamic world of e-commerce, the user experience (UX) on your Shopify store plays a pivotal role in shaping customer satisfaction and influencing purchase decisions. A seamless and user-friendly interface not only attracts visitors but also encourages them to explore, engage, and ultimately make a purchase. This section outlines key strategies to enhance the user experience on your Shopify store, ensuring a positive and intuitive journey for every visitor.

1. **Intuitive Navigation:**

Clear Menu Structure: Design a clear and logically organized menu structure for easy navigation.

Categories and Subcategories: Group products into categories and subcategories, making it effortless for users to find what they're looking for.

2. Streamlined Product Search:

Prominent Search Bar: Place a prominent search bar for users to quickly find specific products.

Autocomplete and Suggestions: Implement autocomplete and intelligent search suggestions for a more efficient search experience.

3. Optimize Product Pages:

Clear Product Descriptions: Craft clear and concise product descriptions that highlight key features and benefits.

High-Quality Images: Feature high-resolution images with zoom functionality for a detailed view.

Customer Reviews: Display customer reviews and ratings to provide social proof and build trust.

4. Responsive Design:

Mobile Optimization: Ensure your Shopify store is optimized for mobile devices, offering a seamless experience on smartphones and tablets.

Cross-Browser Compatibility: Test your store on various browsers to guarantee consistent performance across different platforms.

5. Fast Loading Times:

Image Optimization: Optimize images to reduce loading times without compromising quality.

Minimize HTTP Requests: Streamline your site's design and minimize unnecessary elements to reduce the number of HTTP requests.

6. Guest Checkout Option:

Simplify Checkout Process: Offer a guest checkout option to streamline the purchasing process.

Avoid Mandatory Account Creation: Allow customers to purchase without mandatory account creation to reduce friction.

7. Transparent Policies:

Communicate Policies: Display shipping, return, and refund policies to manage customer expectations.

FAQ Section: Include an FAQ section to address common queries and provide information upfront.

8. Personalization Features:

Product Recommendations: Implement personalized product recommendations based on customer browsing and purchase history.

Dynamic Content: Use dynamic content to tailor the user experience based on individual preferences.

9. Secure Payment Options:

Diverse Payment Methods: Provide a variety of secure payment options to accommodate customer preferences.

SSL Certification: Display SSL certification to assure customers of secure transactions.

10. Customer Support Accessibility:

Live Chat: Offer a live chat feature for real-time assistance.

Contact Information: Provide contact information, including email and a customer support phone number.

11. Multi-Channel Accessibility:

Social Media Integration: Integrate social media links to connect with customers on multiple platforms.

Newsletter Signup: Include an option for newsletter signups to keep customers informed about promotions and updates.

12. A/B Testing:

Test and Iterate: Conduct A/B testing on various elements, such as CTAs, images, or page layouts.

Data-Driven Optimization: Use data from A/B tests to continuously optimize your Shopify store for better performance.

By focusing on these strategies, you can create a Shopify store that not only attracts visitors but also provides a user experience that encourages engagement and conversions. Regularly assess and refine your store based on user feedback and analytics to ensure it evolves with changing customer expectations and industry trends.

Chapter 4: Marketing Strategies for E-commerce Success

In the bustling world of e-commerce, effective marketing strategies are the driving force behind achieving sustainable success and standing out in a crowded marketplace. Chapter 4 is dedicated to unraveling a comprehensive array of marketing strategies tailored for e-commerce businesses. From digital advertising to content marketing and social media campaigns, this chapter guides you through the intricacies of creating a robust marketing plan that not only attracts potential customers but also nurtures lasting relationships and boosts your online store's profitability.

1. **Digital Advertising Domination:**

Dive into the realm of digital advertising, exploring platforms such as Google Ads, Facebook Ads, and Instagram Ads.

Craft compelling ad copies and visuals, targeting specific audience segments to maximize reach and engagement.

Optimize ad campaigns through continuous monitoring, A/B testing, and data-driven refinements.

2. **Content Marketing Mastery:**

Harness the power of content marketing to educate, entertain, and engage your audience.

Develop a blog strategy, creating informative and shareable content related to your industry or products.

Incorporate SEO best practices to enhance your store's visibility on search engines.

3. **Social Media Supremacy:**

Create a strong presence on popular social media platforms, tailoring content to each platform's unique audience.

Implement a social media calendar for consistent posting, incorporating a mix of product highlights, behind-the-scenes glimpses, and user-generated content.

Leverage paid social advertising to amplify your reach and target specific demographics.

4. **Email Marketing Excellence:**

Build and nurture an email subscriber list through incentives, such as discounts or exclusive content.

Develop personalized and engaging email campaigns, including product recommendations, promotions, and newsletters.

Implement segmentation and automation for targeted communication based on customer behavior.

5. **Influencer Collaborations:**

Identify and collaborate with influencers in your niche or industry to leverage their audience.

Foster authentic relationships with influencers who align with your brand values.

Utilize influencer-generated content to showcase your products in real-life scenarios.

6. **Search Engine Optimization (SEO) Strategies:**

Conduct thorough keyword research to optimize product listings and website content.

Focus on on-page SEO elements, including meta tags, alt text, and internal linking.

Monitor and adapt to search engine algorithm changes to maintain high visibility.

7. Loyalty Programs and Customer Retention:

Implement loyalty programs to incentivize repeat purchases and customer loyalty.

Personalize the shopping experience for returning customers through tailored recommendations and exclusive offers.

Solicit and act upon customer feedback to enhance overall satisfaction.

8. Flash Sales and Limited-Time Offers:

Generate excitement and urgency with flash sales and limited-time offers.

Strategically use countdown timers and promotional messaging to drive immediate action.

Monitor inventory and logistics to ensure a seamless execution of time-sensitive promotions.

9. Collaborative Partnerships:

Explore collaboration opportunities with complementary brands or influencers.

Co-create limited-edition products or exclusive bundles to enhance the appeal of collaborative partnerships.

Cross-promote with partners to expand reach and tap into new customer bases.

10. Analytics and Continuous Optimization:

Utilize analytics tools to track the performance of various marketing channels.

Regularly analyze customer behavior, conversion rates, and return on investment (ROI).

Apply insights gained from analytics to continuously optimize and refine your overall marketing strategy.

This chapter serves as a comprehensive guide, offering insights and practical steps to elevate your e-commerce marketing game. From leveraging the potential of digital advertising to building lasting customer relationships through email marketing and loyalty programs, these strategies are designed to propel your online store toward sustained growth and success in the competitive e-commerce landscape.

4.1 Crafting a Winning Marketing Plan

In the dynamic world of e-commerce, a well-crafted marketing plan is the compass that guides your business toward success. Chapter 4 delves into the intricacies of building a comprehensive marketing strategy, incorporating diverse channels to maximize reach, engagement, and conversion rates. This section, in particular, focuses on the fundamental steps involved in creating a winning marketing plan tailored to the unique demands of the online marketplace.

1. **Set Clear Marketing Objectives:**

Define specific and measurable marketing objectives aligned with your overall business goals.

Establish key performance indicators (KPIs) to track the success of your marketing efforts.

2. **Know Your Target Audience:**

Conduct thorough market research to understand the demographics, preferences, and behaviors of your target audience.

Create detailed customer personas to tailor your marketing messages effectively.

3. **Select Your Marketing Channels:**

Identify and prioritize the most relevant marketing channels for your business, considering factors such as your target audience's online behavior and your product offerings.

Channels may include digital advertising (Google Ads, Facebook Ads), content marketing, social media, email marketing, and influencer collaborations.

4. **Develop a Budget and Allocation Strategy:**

Allocate your marketing budget based on the channels that align with your objectives and audience.

Consider a mix of paid and organic strategies, adjusting allocations based on performance.

5. **Craft Compelling Content:**

Develop a content strategy that aligns with your brand voice and resonates with your target audience.

Create diverse content types, including blog posts, videos, infographics, and social media posts.

6. **Implement SEO Best Practices:**

Optimize your website and product pages for search engines by incorporating relevant keywords and ensuring proper Meta tags.

Create a robust backlink strategy to enhance your site's authority.

7. Build a Social Media Calendar:

Create a social media calendar outlining your content schedule across various platforms.

Tailor your content for each platform, considering the unique characteristics and audience expectations.

8. Execute Paid Advertising Campaigns:

Launch targeted paid advertising campaigns on platforms like Google Ads and social media channels.

Set clear goals for each campaign, whether it's increasing brand awareness, driving traffic, or boosting conversions.

9. Leverage Email Marketing:

Build and segment your email subscriber list for personalized communication.

Develop automated email campaigns for onboarding, abandoned carts, and post-purchase follow-ups.

10. Monitor, Analyze, and Adjust:

Utilize analytics tools to monitor the performance of each marketing channel.

Regularly analyze data to understand customer behavior, conversion rates, and ROI.

Use insights to make informed adjustments and optimizations to your marketing plan.

11. Incorporate Customer Feedback:

Encourage and collect customer feedback to understand their experience with your brand.

Use feedback to refine your marketing messages, product offerings, and overall customer experience.

12. Stay Agile and Adapt:

Stay informed about industry trends, emerging technologies, and changes in consumer behavior.

Be agile in adapting your marketing plan to seize new opportunities and address evolving challenges.

By diligently following these steps, your e-commerce business can create a robust and adaptable marketing plan. This plan serves as a dynamic roadmap, guiding your efforts to reach, engage, and convert your target audience effectively in the ever-evolving digital landscape.

4.2 Leveraging Social Media for Maximum Impact

In the contemporary e-commerce landscape, social media stands as a dynamic powerhouse for connecting with your audience, building brand awareness, and driving conversions. This section explores the intricacies of leveraging social media platforms to their fullest potential, outlining strategies to maximize impact and cultivate a vibrant online presence.

1. **Platform Selection and Audience Insight:**

Identify the social media platforms most relevant to your target audience. Consider factors such as demographics, user behavior, and platform features.

Leverage analytics tools to gain insights into audience preferences, allowing you to tailor content effectively.

2. **Tailored Content Creation:**

Develop a content strategy that aligns with your brand identity and resonates with your audience.

Craft a mix of content types, including visually appealing images, engaging videos, informative infographics, and compelling written posts.

3. **Consistent Brand Voice:**

Establish a consistent brand voice across all social media platforms. Ensure that your tone, messaging, and visual elements align with your brand identity.

Cultivate a personality that connects with your audience authentically.

4. **Engaging Visuals and Multimedia:**

Prioritize high-quality visuals and multimedia content to capture attention in crowded feeds.

Utilize Instagram, Facebook, and Pinterest for visually-driven content, while incorporating video content on platforms like TikTok and YouTube.

5. **Social Media Advertising:**

Explore paid advertising options on platforms like Facebook Ads, Instagram Ads, and Twitter Ads.

Define specific campaign objectives, target audiences, and budgets to maximize the effectiveness of your ad spend.

6. **Influencer Collaborations:**

Identify and collaborate with influencers whose audience aligns with your target demographic.

Foster authentic partnerships that showcase your products or services in a genuine and relatable manner.

7. **Community Building and Engagement:**

Actively engage with your audience through comments, direct messages, and polls.

Foster a sense of community by encouraging user-generated content, hosting giveaways, and acknowledging customer contributions.

8. **Social Media Analytics and Insights:**

Utilize analytics tools provided by each platform to track the performance of your social media efforts.

Monitor metrics such as engagement rates, click-through rates, and follower growth to assess the effectiveness of your strategies.

9. **Strategic Posting Schedule:**

Develop a posting schedule that aligns with the peak activity times of your target audience.

Experiment with different posting frequencies and timings to identify the optimal schedule for maximum visibility.

10. Cross-Promotion and Collaborations:

Explore cross-promotional opportunities with other brands or influencers in your niche.

Collaborate on joint campaigns, takeovers, or shared content to expand your reach.

11. Storytelling and Behind-the-Scenes:

Embrace storytelling to humanize your brand and connect with your audience on a personal level.

Share behind-the-scenes glimpses, company milestones, and stories that resonate with your brand values.

12. Crisis Management and Responsiveness:

Establish a crisis management plan to address any negative publicity or social media crises promptly.

Respond to customer inquiries and feedback promptly, demonstrating transparency and accountability.

By strategically employing these social media tactics, your e-commerce business can harness the full potential of these platforms, fostering brand loyalty, driving traffic to your store, and ultimately boosting conversions. Social media becomes not just a promotional tool but a dynamic avenue for building meaningful connections with your audience in the digital realm.

4.3 Implementing Effective Email Marketing Campaigns

Email marketing remains a powerful tool in the arsenal of e-commerce businesses, enabling direct communication with your audience and nurturing lasting relationships. This section delves into the key strategies for implementing effective email marketing campaigns that resonate with your subscribers, drive engagement, and contribute to overall business success.

1. **Build and Segment Your Email List:**

Develop a robust subscriber list by implementing sign-up forms on your website, leveraging pop-ups, and offering incentives for newsletter subscriptions.

Segment your list based on demographics, purchase history, and engagement levels to deliver personalized content.

2. Personalized and Targeted Campaigns:

Craft personalized email campaigns that speak directly to the needs and preferences of specific customer segments.

Leverage data to send targeted campaigns, such as abandoned cart emails, product recommendations, and exclusive promotions.

3. Compelling Email Content:

Create engaging and valuable content that captures the attention of your subscribers.

Experiment with various content types, including product highlights, educational content, and user-generated stories.

4. Responsive Design and Mobile Optimization:

Ensure your emails are mobile-friendly, with responsive designs that adapt seamlessly to various screen sizes.

Optimize images and content to load quickly on mobile devices, enhancing the user experience.

5. **Strategic Timing and Frequency:**

Experiment with different send times and frequencies to identify the optimal schedule for your audience.

Consider time zones and the nature of your content when determining the timing of your campaigns.

6. **Compelling Subject Lines:**

Craft compelling and concise subject lines that entice subscribers to open your emails.

A/B test different subject lines to understand what resonates most with your audience.

7. **Incorporate Calls-to-Action (CTAs):**

Include CTAs that guide subscribers towards desired actions, whether it's making a purchase, exploring new products, or engaging with your content.

Use contrasting colors and persuasive language to make CTAs stand out.

8. **Automate Email Campaigns:**

Implement automation for key touchpoints in the customer journey, such as welcome emails, post-purchase follow-ups, and re-engagement campaigns.

Use triggers based on subscriber behavior to deliver timely and relevant messages.

9. Monitor and Analyze Performance:

Utilize email analytics tools to track the performance of your campaigns.

Monitor metrics such as open rates, click-through rates, and conversion rates to assess the effectiveness of your email marketing efforts.

10. A/B Testing for Optimization:

Conduct A/B testing on different elements of your emails, including headlines, visuals, and CTAs.

Use insights from A/B tests to refine and optimize your future email campaigns.

11. Customer Feedback and Surveys:

Solicit feedback from your subscribers through surveys or direct inquiries.

Use customer input to tailor future campaigns, address concerns, and enhance overall satisfaction.

12. Compliance with Email Regulations:

Familiarize yourself with and adhere to email marketing regulations, including GDPR and the CAN-SPAM Act.

Ensure that subscribers have the option to opt out and that your email practices align with privacy guidelines.

By incorporating these strategies into your email marketing endeavors, your e-commerce business can cultivate a more engaged subscriber base, drive customer loyalty, and contribute to the overall success of your online store. Email marketing, when executed thoughtfully, serves as a personalized and effective communication channel to connect with your audience throughout their customer journey.

Chapter 5: Maximizing Profits with Shopify

In the fifth chapter of our guide, we delve into the intricacies of leveraging Shopify to its fullest potential, aiming not just for operational efficiency but for the maximization of profits. This chapter serves as a comprehensive manual, offering detailed insights and actionable strategies to fine-tune your Shopify store and optimize revenue streams. From advanced marketing techniques to strategic product placement, we explore every facet that contributes to the bottom line of your e-commerce venture.

1. **Advanced Marketing Tactics:**

Uncover advanced digital marketing strategies tailored for Shopify, including retargeting campaigns, lookalike audiences, and advanced segmentation.

Harness the power of data analytics to identify high-value customer segments, enabling targeted and personalized marketing efforts.

2. **Conversion Rate Optimization (CRO):**

Dive into the nuances of CRO, exploring techniques to optimize your website for higher conversion rates.

Implement A/B testing on product pages, checkout processes, and CTAs to fine-tune elements that directly impact conversion.

3. Upselling and Cross-Selling Strategies:

Implement effective upselling and cross-selling techniques within the Shopify platform to increase average order value.

Leverage product bundling, personalized recommendations, and strategic placement of related items to encourage additional purchases.

4. Inventory Management for Profitability:

Fine-tune your inventory management processes to minimize overstock or stockouts, ensuring a healthy balance between supply and demand.

Implement dynamic pricing strategies based on demand fluctuations, seasonal trends, and competitor analysis.

5. Implementing Subscription Models:

Explore the integration of subscription-based models into your Shopify store, fostering recurring revenue streams.

Design enticing subscription offers, coupled with personalized experiences, to encourage long-term customer commitment.

6. Exclusive Promotions and Loyalty Programs:

Strategically deploy exclusive promotions and loyalty programs to reward repeat customers and incentivize brand loyalty.

Utilize Shopify's built-in tools for loyalty points, discounts, and VIP programs to create a compelling customer retention strategy.

7. Streamlining Checkout Processes:

Optimize the checkout process to minimize friction and cart abandonment.

Implement one-click checkouts, guest checkout options, and transparent shipping information to enhance the overall customer experience.

8. Data-Driven Decision Making:

Embrace a data-driven approach to decision-making, utilizing Shopify's analytics and reporting tools.

Analyze customer behavior, product performance, and sales trends to inform strategic business decisions for increased profitability.

9. Expanding Product Catalog Responsibly:

Strategically expand your product catalog by introducing complementary products or exploring new niches.

Conduct thorough market research and assess customer demand to ensure the viability and profitability of new additions.

10. Outsourcing and Automation:

Explore outsourcing options and automation tools within the Shopify ecosystem to streamline business operations.

Delegate routine tasks to focus on high-impact activities that directly contribute to profit maximization.

11. Customer Retention and Lifetime Value:

Develop robust customer retention strategies to increase customer lifetime value.

Implement post-purchase engagement, personalized communication, and proactive customer support to foster lasting relationships.

12. Regulatory Compliance and Risk Management:

Navigate regulatory compliance within the e-commerce landscape to mitigate potential risks.

Implement robust risk management practices, including secure payment gateways, data protection measures, and adherence to industry standards.

This chapter serves as a comprehensive guide to not only navigate the Shopify platform effectively but also to strategically align your business operations for profit maximization. By implementing these detailed strategies, your Shopify store can transcend from a mere storefront to a profit-generating engine in the competitive e-commerce arena.

5.1 Pricing Strategies for Increased Revenue

In the pursuit of maximizing revenue within your Shopify store, strategic pricing stands as a pivotal element that directly influences customer behavior and overall profitability. This section explores diverse pricing strategies tailored for e-commerce businesses, providing insights into how you can fine-tune your pricing model to attract customers, boost sales, and enhance your bottom line.

1. **Dynamic Pricing Tactics:**

Embrace dynamic pricing by adjusting product prices based on real-time factors such as demand, competitor pricing, and inventory levels.

Implement intelligent algorithms or use Shopify apps to automate dynamic pricing, ensuring competitiveness in the market.

2. **Discount and Promotional Pricing:**

Strategically deploy discounts and promotional pricing to stimulate customer interest and drive sales.

Consider limited-time offers, flash sales, and seasonal promotions to create a sense of urgency and incentivize purchases.

3. **Tiered Pricing Structures:**

Introduce tiered pricing structures that encourage customers to buy in larger quantities.

Create graduated pricing tiers where the per-unit cost decreases as customers purchase higher quantities of a product.

4. **Bundle and Package Pricing:**

Increase average order value by offering bundled products at a discounted rate.

Create packages that combine related items, providing customers with value while boosting overall revenue.

5. **Subscription-Based Models:**

Explore the implementation of subscription-based pricing models, fostering recurring revenue streams.

Provide subscription options for consumable or regularly replenished products, ensuring a steady flow of income.

6. **Psychological Pricing Strategies:**

Leverage psychological pricing techniques, such as pricing products at $9.99 instead of $10.00.

Experiment with pricing endings, decimals, and round numbers to influence customer perceptions.

7. **Value-Based Pricing:**

Set prices based on the perceived value of your products or services rather than solely on production costs.

Highlight unique features, quality, or additional services to justify higher prices for premium offerings.

8. **Anchor Pricing Techniques:**

Implement anchor pricing by showcasing a higher-priced product first, making subsequent options appear more affordable.

Use anchor pricing in conjunction with discounts or promotions to enhance perceived value.

9. **Geographic and Segmented Pricing:**

Consider adjusting prices based on geographic locations, taking into account varying market conditions and customer purchasing power.

Implement segmented pricing for different customer groups, tailoring prices to specific demographics or loyalty levels.

10. **Penetration Pricing Strategies:**

Employ penetration pricing for new product launches to quickly capture market share.

Gradually adjust prices upwards as the product establishes itself in the market.

11. **Responsive Pricing to Competitors:**

Monitor competitor pricing and adjust your prices to remain competitive.

Utilize Shopify apps or external tools to track competitor pricing changes and inform your pricing strategy.

12. **Data-Driven Price Optimization:**

Leverage data analytics within Shopify to continuously optimize pricing based on customer behavior, sales trends, and overall market dynamics.

Regularly assess the performance of different pricing strategies and iterate based on data insights.

By strategically incorporating these pricing strategies, your Shopify store can navigate the complexities of the e-commerce landscape, attract diverse customer segments, and ultimately increase revenue. The key lies in a dynamic approach, utilizing data-driven insights and staying responsive to market changes to ensure sustained profitability and competitiveness.

5.2 Implementing Upsells and Cross-Sells: Elevating Your Sales Strategy

Unlocking the potential for increased revenue within your Shopify store involves mastering the art of upselling and cross-selling. These strategic techniques go beyond mere transactions; they craft a dynamic and personalized shopping experience that not only meets but exceeds customer expectations. In the realm of upselling, consider employing intelligent algorithms and Shopify apps to recommend complementary or upgraded products strategically. Showcase premium alternatives, enticing customers to explore enhanced options during their purchase journey. Concurrently, cross-selling techniques seamlessly weave related products into the customer experience. Create bundled product offerings, featuring items frequently bought together, and strategically present these options both pre and post-purchase. Harness customer data to deliver personalized recommendations, ensuring that the suggestions align with individual preferences and purchase history.

To incentivize bundled purchases, offer exclusive deals or discounts, and encourage customers to add more items to their carts. Timely upsell offers can be introduced on the checkout page, prompting customers to enhance their order before finalizing their purchase. Post-purchase upsell emails serve as an effective follow-up strategy, suggesting additional products that complement their recent acquisition. Tiered pricing structures and quantity-based discounts incentivize customers to buy in larger quantities, while upgraded or premium versions of products present enticing options. The creation of appealing product bundles, curated based on themes or occasions, adds a layer of excitement to the shopping experience. Implementing limited-time bundle offers infuses a sense of urgency, encouraging customers to capitalize on exclusive deals.

A seamless shopping experience is paramount to the success of upselling and cross-selling. Ensure that recommendations integrate effortlessly into the shopping journey, avoiding disruption. Clear communication of the value and benefits of upsell or cross-sell items is crucial for customer understanding and satisfaction. Educate customers through informative product descriptions and engaging content that highlights the advantages of upgrading or adding complementary products. Testing and optimization are key components of a successful strategy. Conduct A/B testing on different approaches to identify what resonates best with your audience, and iteratively optimize based on customer feedback and performance metrics.

Integrating upselling and cross-selling into your loyalty program can further enhance customer engagement. Reward points for upsells or offer exclusive deals to loyalty program members, creating an added layer of incentive for repeat customers. The strategic placement and visibility of upsell and cross-sell suggestions on product pages and during the checkout process ensure that these opportunities are easily noticed and accessible across various devices.

In summary, the implementation of upselling and cross-selling techniques is not just about boosting transaction values; it's about sculpting a customer-centric approach that adds significant value to each shopping experience. By seamlessly incorporating these strategies into your Shopify store, you not only elevate your sales game but also cultivate a loyal customer base that appreciates the personalized and curated nature of their interactions with your brand.

5.3 Streamlining Your Order Fulfillment Process

Efficient order fulfillment is the lifeblood of an e-commerce business, directly impacting customer satisfaction and operational success. To achieve a streamlined process within the Shopify ecosystem, consider the following strategies:

Optimizing Inventory Management:

Efficient order fulfillment begins with accurate inventory management. Implement real-time inventory tracking to provide customers with up-to-date product availability information. Automated restocking alerts ensure timely replenishment, reducing the risk of stockouts and enhancing customer trust.

Automating Order Processing:

Leverage Shopify's order management apps to automate routine tasks like order confirmation emails and processing. Batch processing orders improves efficiency, allowing for a more organized and time-effective approach to handling multiple orders simultaneously.

Seamless Integration with Shipping Carriers:

Integrate Shopify with shipping carriers to streamline label generation and order tracking. Automated shipping notifications keep customers informed about the status of their orders, contributing to a positive post-purchase experience.

Efficient Pick, Pack, and Ship Operations:

Optimize warehouse layout for efficiency, ensuring products are easily accessible for picking. Implement barcode scanning technology to minimize errors during the picking and packing stages, enhancing overall accuracy.

Multi-Warehouse Management Strategies:

Consider a multi-warehouse strategy to reduce shipping distances and improve delivery speed. Distribute inventory across multiple warehouses based on geographical demand patterns to enhance operational efficiency.

Enhanced Order Tracking for Customers:

Provide customers with order tracking pages for real-time monitoring of their shipments. Automated tracking emails keep customers informed and reduce inquiries about order status, contributing to a smoother customer experience.

Cost-Effective Shipping Solutions:

Negotiate competitive shipping rates with carriers to minimize shipping costs. Implement smart packaging solutions to optimize packaging and reduce dimensional weight charges.

Efficient Returns and Exchanges Handling:

Communicate return policies on your Shopify store to manage customer expectations. Implement automated returns processing to expedite the handling of returned items, ensuring a smooth process for both customers and the business.

Effective Customer Communication Systems:

Keep customers informed about any delays or issues with their orders through proactive communication. Integrate customer support channels within Shopify for seamless issue resolution and communication, enhancing overall customer satisfaction.

Continuous Monitoring and Improvement:

Utilize analytics tools to monitor key performance metrics, including order fulfillment times and error rates. Continuously analyze data and customer feedback to identify areas for improvement and optimize the order fulfillment process iteratively.

Employee Training and Engagement Initiatives:

Provide comprehensive training programs for fulfillment staff to ensure they are well-versed in efficient order processing. Foster a positive and engaged workforce to enhance productivity and accuracy in the fulfillment process.

Integration with ERP Systems for Holistic Coordination:

Integrate Shopify with Enterprise Resource Planning (ERP) systems for seamless coordination between order fulfillment, inventory management, and other business processes. Automated data syncing ensures accurate and up-to-date information, facilitating a holistic and efficient operational approach.

By implementing these strategies, your Shopify store can achieve a well-orchestrated and effective order fulfillment process, paving the way for enhanced customer satisfaction, operational efficiency, and overall business success.

Chapter 6: Analytics and Insights

In the rapidly evolving realm of e-commerce, leveraging analytics and insights is not just an option; it's a strategic imperative. This chapter delves into the multifaceted world of data-driven decision-making within the Shopify ecosystem, offering a comprehensive guide on how to harness analytics to optimize every facet of your online business.

1. **Understanding Key Performance Indicators (KPIs):**

Sales Metrics: Dive into crucial sales metrics such as revenue, average order value (AOV), and conversion rates. Track sales performance over time to identify trends and patterns.

Customer Acquisition Cost (CAC): Calculate the cost of acquiring a customer through various channels to evaluate the effectiveness of marketing efforts.

Customer Lifetime Value (CLV): Gauge the long-term value of a customer to inform marketing and retention strategies.

2. **Google Analytics Integration:**

Setting Up Google Analytics: Integrate Google Analytics with your Shopify store to access comprehensive data on user behavior, traffic sources, and website performance.

Utilizing E-commerce Tracking: Leverage e-commerce tracking features to gain insights into product performance, sales attribution, and customer journey analysis.

3. **Shopify Analytics Dashboard:**

Navigating Shopify's Native Analytics: Explore Shopify's built-in analytics dashboard for a quick overview of key metrics. Understand trends in sales, customer behavior, and inventory performance.

Sales Channel Analysis: Evaluate the performance of different sales channels, including online stores, social media, and third-party marketplaces.

4. **Advanced Segmentation for Targeted Insights:**

Customer Segmentation: Utilize advanced segmentation to categorize customers based on demographics, purchase history, and behavior. Tailor marketing strategies to specific customer segments for personalized engagement.

Product Segmentation: Analyze product performance by segmenting items based on categories, pricing tiers, or popularity. Optimize inventory and marketing strategies accordingly.

5. **Conversion Funnel Analysis:**

Mapping the Customer Journey: Visualize the customer journey from awareness to conversion using conversion funnels. Identify potential bottlenecks or areas for improvement in the purchase process.

Abandoned Cart Analysis: Investigate and address factors leading to abandoned carts by analyzing user behavior during the checkout process.

6. **Behavioral Analytics for User Insights:**

Heatmaps and Session Recordings: Implement tools like heatmaps and session recordings to understand how users interact with your website. Identify popular areas, navigation patterns, and potential friction points.

User Flow Analysis: Examine the flow of user interactions on your site to identify common paths, drop-off points, and areas for optimization.

7. A/B Testing for Continuous Improvement:

Designing A/B Tests: Implement A/B testing on various elements of your Shopify store, such as product pages, CTAs, and promotional banners. Evaluate performance variations to make informed design and content decisions.

Iterative Optimization: Continuously iterate based on A/B test results to refine the user experience and enhance conversion rates.

8. Social Media Analytics:

Social Media Engagement Metrics: Monitor social media metrics such as likes, shares, and comments to assess the impact of your social media campaigns.

Referral Traffic Analysis: Track traffic from social media channels to your Shopify store. Identify high-performing platforms and tailor social media strategies accordingly.

9. Email Marketing Analytics:

Open and Click-Through Rates: Analyze email campaign performance through metrics like open and click-through rates. Optimize email content and design based on user engagement.

Conversion Tracking: Implement conversion tracking in email campaigns to measure the impact on sales and customer acquisition.

10. Customer Feedback and Reviews Analysis:

Review Aggregation Platforms: Utilize review aggregation platforms to monitor customer feedback and sentiment. Address issues highlighted in reviews and leverage positive feedback for marketing.

Surveys and Feedback Forms: Implement surveys and feedback forms to gather direct insights from customers. Use the data to refine products, services, and the overall shopping experience.

11. Predictive Analytics for Future Trends:

Demand Forecasting: Leverage predictive analytics for demand forecasting. Anticipate future trends, optimize inventory levels, and stay ahead of market shifts.

Personalized Recommendations: Implement machine learning algorithms to offer personalized product recommendations based on customer preferences and behavior.

12. Privacy and Compliance:

GDPR and Data Privacy: Ensure compliance with data protection regulations such as GDPR. Prioritize customer privacy and transparently communicate data usage policies.

Secure Data Handling: Implement secure data handling practices to protect customer information. Utilize secure payment gateways and encryption methods for transactional data.

In conclusion, navigating the data landscape in the e-commerce domain is not merely about collecting information but about deriving actionable insights to propel your business forward. By mastering analytics within the Shopify ecosystem, you equip yourself with the tools to optimize marketing strategies, enhance user experiences, and make informed decisions that contribute to sustained growth and success in the competitive online marketplace.

6.1 Utilizing Shopify Analytics Tools

In the dynamic landscape of e-commerce, harnessing the power of data is a game-changer, and Shopify provides a robust set of analytics tools to empower merchants in making informed decisions. This section delves into the key features and functionalities within the Shopify Analytics suite, offering insights into how businesses can leverage these tools to gain a deeper understanding of their performance and enhance overall efficiency.

1. Shopify Analytics Dashboard:

Overview of Key Metrics: The native analytics dashboard within Shopify offers a centralized hub for tracking fundamental metrics such as sales, orders, and average order value. Merchants can quickly grasp the health of their business at a glance.

Sales Channel Analysis: Dive deeper into the performance of different sales channels, including the online store, social media, and third-party marketplaces. This allows businesses to identify high-performing channels and allocate resources strategically.

2. Sales Reports:

Detailed Sales Insights: Shopify's sales reports provide comprehensive insights into sales performance over different periods. Merchants can analyze trends, identify peak sales times, and assess the impact of promotions.

Product Performance Analysis: Drill down into product-specific data, examining which items are top sellers, their contribution to overall revenue, and any seasonal variations.

3. Customer Reports:

Customer Segmentation: Shopify's customer reports enable businesses to segment their customer base based on various criteria such as demographics, location, and purchase history. This segmentation facilitates targeted marketing efforts.

Customer Lifetime Value (CLV): Gain a holistic view of customer value over time, helping businesses understand the long-term impact of customer acquisition and tailor retention strategies accordingly.

4. Acquisition and Behavior Reports:

Traffic Sources Analysis: Identify the sources driving traffic to your Shopify store, whether it be direct visits, organic searches, or referral links. This data aids in optimizing marketing strategies.

Conversion Funnel Tracking: Visualize the customer journey through conversion funnels, pinpointing areas of drop-off or friction in the purchasing process. This information is invaluable for refining the user experience.

5. Custom Reports and Segmentation:

Tailored Data Analysis: Shopify allows merchants to create custom reports, tailoring analytics to suit specific business needs. This flexibility ensures businesses can focus on the metrics most relevant to their goals.

Advanced Segmentation: Utilize advanced segmentation to categorize customers, products, or orders based on specific criteria. This enables businesses to derive nuanced insights and inform targeted strategies.

6. Financial Reports:

Profit and Loss Statements: Shopify's financial reports provide a snapshot of the business's financial health, including revenue, expenses, and profits. This information aids in budgeting and financial planning.

Tax Reporting: Streamline tax-related processes by leveraging financial reports that break down tax-related transactions and calculations.

7. Inventory Reports:

Stock Level Monitoring: Keep a close eye on inventory with Shopify's inventory reports, which provide real-time insights into stock levels, product popularity, and sales velocity. This aids in avoiding stockouts and overstock situations.

Product Performance Analytics: Evaluate the performance of individual products, identifying those that contribute most significantly to sales and adjusting inventory strategies accordingly.

8. Time-Based Analytics:

Seasonal Analysis: Use time-based analytics to understand seasonal trends and capitalize on peak periods. Merchants can align marketing efforts, promotions, and inventory management with seasonal demand fluctuations.

Performance Benchmarking: Compare performance metrics across different periods to assess growth, identify patterns, and make data-driven decisions for the future.

9. Reporting Automation:

Scheduled Reports: Shopify allows merchants to automate the delivery of key reports via email. This ensures that stakeholders receive timely insights without the need for manual data retrieval.

Data Export Capability: Export data for further analysis or integration with external tools, providing flexibility for businesses with specific reporting requirements.

In summary, Shopify's analytics tools serve as a compass in the data landscape, guiding businesses toward actionable insights that fuel strategic decision-making. By embracing and effectively utilizing these tools, merchants can unravel the intricacies of their e-commerce operations, optimize performance, and pave the way for sustained growth in the competitive online marketplace.

6.2 Interpreting Key E-commerce Metrics

In the realm of e-commerce, success hinges on the ability to decipher and derive meaningful insights from an array of key metrics. This section provides a comprehensive exploration of pivotal e-commerce metrics, shedding light on their interpretation within the Shopify framework. By understanding and interpreting these metrics, businesses can unravel the narrative of their performance and take informed actions to propel their online ventures to new heights.

1. **Conversion Rate:**

Definition: The conversion rate is the percentage of website visitors who complete a desired action, such as making a purchase.

Interpretation: A high conversion rate indicates effective marketing, compelling product pages, and a smooth checkout process. Conversely, a low rate may highlight potential issues in these areas.

2. **Average Order Value (AOV):**

Definition: AOV represents the average amount spent by a customer in a single transaction.

Interpretation: Monitoring AOV provides insights into customer spending habits. An increasing AOV suggests successful upselling or cross-selling strategies, while a decreasing AOV may require a reassessment of pricing or promotion strategies.

3. **Customer Acquisition Cost (CAC):**

Definition: CAC measures the cost of acquiring a new customer, factoring in marketing and advertising expenses.

Interpretation: A lower CAC is favorable, indicating efficient marketing spend. A rising CAC may necessitate a reassessment of acquisition channels or marketing strategies.

4. Customer Lifetime Value (CLV):

Definition: CLV estimates the total revenue a business can expect from a customer over their entire relationship.

Interpretation: A high CLV indicates strong customer loyalty and the potential for long-term profitability. Businesses should aim to exceed their CAC with the CLV for sustainable growth.

5. Cart Abandonment Rate:

Definition: Cart abandonment rate measures the percentage of users who add items to their cart but do not complete the purchase.

Interpretation: A high abandonment rate may signal issues in the checkout process or shipping costs. Reducing friction points and implementing retargeting strategies can help lower this rate.

6. Return on Advertising Spend (ROAS):

Definition: ROAS quantifies the revenue generated for every dollar spent on advertising.

Interpretation: A ROAS above 1 indicates a profitable advertising campaign, while a lower ROAS may necessitate adjustments to ad targeting, messaging, or platforms.

7. Inventory Turnover:

Definition: Inventory turnover measures how quickly a business sells and replaces its inventory within a specific timeframe.

Interpretation: High inventory turnover suggests efficient stock management, while low turnover may indicate overstock issues. Balancing inventory levels with demand is crucial for profitability.

8. Website Traffic and Source Analysis:

Definition: Analyzing website traffic includes understanding the number of visitors and their sources (organic, direct, referral, or social).

Interpretation: A diverse traffic mix is desirable. A surge in organic traffic reflects effective SEO, while a high bounce rate may indicate issues with site content or user experience.

9. Refund Rate:

Definition: The refund rate represents the percentage of orders that result in a refund.

Interpretation: A lower refund rate signifies customer satisfaction, while a high rate may indicate product quality issues or discrepancies between expectations and reality.

10. Abandoned Checkout Recovery:

Definition: This metric tracks the success rate of recovering abandoned carts through retargeting or automated email campaigns.

Interpretation: A high recovery rate implies effective strategies to re-engage potential customers. Optimizing email content and timing can further enhance recovery efforts.

11. Social Media Engagement:

Definition: Social media metrics encompass likes, shares, comments, and click-through rates on platforms where the business is active.

Interpretation: Engagement metrics gauge the effectiveness of social media efforts. High engagement signifies a strong social media presence, while low engagement may necessitate content adjustments.

12. Mobile Conversion Rate:

Definition: This metric specifically measures the conversion rate of visitors using mobile devices.

Interpretation: A high mobile conversion rate indicates a mobile-friendly site, while a lower rate may prompt businesses to optimize their mobile experience.

In essence, interpreting these key e-commerce metrics is akin to deciphering the language of success in the digital marketplace. By scrutinizing these indicators within the Shopify ecosystem, businesses can uncover actionable insights, refine strategies, and chart a course for sustained growth in the ever-evolving world of online commerce.

6.3 Making Data-Driven Decisions for Growth

In the fast-paced and data-rich landscape of e-commerce, the ability to make informed decisions based on data analysis is a cornerstone of sustainable growth. This section explores the principles and strategies behind making data-driven decisions within the Shopify framework, emphasizing the pivotal role of analytics in steering businesses toward success.

1. **Define Clear Objectives:**

Align with Business Goals: Before delving into data, clearly define your business objectives. Whether it's increasing revenue, optimizing marketing spend, or enhancing customer retention, aligning data analysis with overarching goals is crucial.

Identify Key Performance Indicators (KPIs): Determine the specific metrics that directly contribute to your defined objectives. This could include conversion rates, customer acquisition costs, or inventory turnover, depending on your business priorities.

2. **Leverage Shopify Analytics Tools:**

Explore Native Features: Familiarize yourself with Shopify's native analytics tools. The dashboard, sales reports, and customer insights provided by Shopify offer a foundational understanding of your e-commerce performance.

Custom Reports and Segmentation: Dive deeper by creating custom reports and leveraging segmentation features. Tailoring your analysis to specific aspects of your business allows for more nuanced insights.

3. Continuous Monitoring and Iteration:

Real-Time Analysis: Embrace real-time analytics to monitor ongoing campaigns and strategies. This enables timely adjustments based on emerging trends or unexpected challenges.

Iterative Optimization: Use data to inform iterative optimization. Regularly revisit and refine strategies based on performance metrics, ensuring continuous improvement in your e-commerce operations.

4. Conversion Rate Optimization (CRO):

Identify Conversion Bottlenecks: Analyze conversion funnels to identify potential bottlenecks in the customer journey. Pinpoint stages with high drop-off rates and implement optimizations to streamline the process.

A/B Testing: Implement A/B testing on elements influencing conversion rates, such as product pages, CTAs, or checkout processes. Data from A/B tests provides insights into what resonates best with your audience.

5. Customer Segmentation Strategies:

Behavioral Segmentation: Leverage behavioral segmentation to categorize customers based on their interactions with your store. Tailor marketing strategies to specific segments, delivering more personalized and effective campaigns.

Product Segmentation: Analyze product performance by segmenting items based on categories, pricing tiers, or popularity. Adjust inventory and marketing strategies to align with the unique attributes of each product segment.

6. **Forecasting and Planning:**

Demand Forecasting: Utilize data for demand forecasting to anticipate trends and seasonal variations. This aids in proactive inventory management and ensures sufficient stock levels during peak periods.

Budget Planning: Data-driven insights inform budget allocation for marketing, advertising, and other operational expenses. Allocate resources based on channels or strategies that yield the highest return on investment.

7. **Customer Feedback and Reviews Analysis:**

Feedback Platforms: Monitor customer feedback platforms and reviews for insights into product satisfaction and pain points. Address issues highlighted by customers and leverage positive feedback for marketing.

Surveys and Direct Feedback: Implement surveys or direct feedback mechanisms to gather insights directly from customers. Use this data to enhance products, services, and the overall customer experience.

8. Social Media and Email Marketing Optimization:

Social Media Analytics: Analyze social media metrics to understand engagement and the impact of social campaigns. Adjust content and posting strategies based on platforms that drive the most traffic.

Email Campaign Performance: Evaluate email marketing performance through open and click-through rates. Optimize campaigns based on data, segmenting audiences for more targeted communication.

9. Competitor Analysis:

Benchmarking: Compare your performance metrics with industry benchmarks and competitors. This provides context for your data and highlights areas where you may need to catch up or differentiate.

Identify Industry Trends: Analyzing competitor strategies and industry trends helps you stay ahead of the curve. Data-driven insights gleaned from this analysis inform strategic decisions and keep your business agile.

10. Data Privacy and Compliance:

Secure Data Handling: Prioritize data privacy and implement secure data handling practices. Adhere to regulations such as GDPR to maintain customer trust and comply with legal requirements.

Transparent Communication: Communicate transparently with customers about data usage policies. Establish trust by clearly outlining how customer data is handled and protected.

In conclusion, making data-driven decisions for growth within the Shopify ecosystem involves a strategic combination of analysis, optimization, and adaptability. By weaving data into the fabric of your decision-making processes, your e-commerce business can navigate the complexities of the digital marketplace with agility, capitalize on opportunities, and chart a course toward sustained success and expansion.

Chapter 7: Scaling Your E-commerce Business

Scaling an e-commerce business is not just about growth in numbers; it's a strategic evolution that demands careful planning, execution, and adaptability. In this chapter, we explore the essential elements and proven strategies for scaling your e-commerce venture within the Shopify ecosystem. From operational optimizations to marketing strategies, this guide is designed to empower businesses on their journey to sustainable and profitable expansion.

1. **Operational Efficiency and Automation:**

Inventory Management: Implement advanced inventory management systems to optimize stock levels, reduce holding costs, and ensure products are readily available to meet increasing demand.

Order Fulfillment Automation: Streamline order fulfillment processes by integrating automation tools. This includes automated order processing, label generation, and efficient pick, pack, and ship operations.

2. **Scalable Technology Infrastructure:**

Evaluate Hosting Solutions: Assess your hosting infrastructure to ensure it can handle increased traffic and transactions. Consider scalable hosting solutions to accommodate growing demands without compromising website performance.

Optimize Website Speed: Enhance website speed and performance to provide a seamless and responsive user experience. Fast-loading pages contribute to higher conversion rates and customer satisfaction.

3. **Expanding Product Offerings:**

Diversify Product Range: Explore opportunities to expand your product range. Conduct market research to identify complementary or trending products that align with your brand, attracting a broader customer base.

Introduce Product Bundles: Create product bundles and packages to encourage upsells and increase the average order value. This strategy enhances customer value while driving additional revenue.

4. **International Expansion:**

Evaluate Global Market Opportunities: Assess the viability of entering international markets. Research and identify regions where there is demand for your products and adapt your strategy to cater to diverse consumer preferences.

Localized Marketing and Content: Tailor marketing efforts and website content to resonate with different cultures and languages. This includes localized product descriptions, currency options, and region-specific promotions.

5. **Customer Retention Strategies:**

Implement Loyalty Programs: Introduce customer loyalty programs to incentivize repeat purchases. Reward customers for their loyalty with exclusive discounts, early access to new products, or redeemable points.

Personalized Marketing Campaigns: Leverage customer data to create personalized marketing campaigns. Send targeted emails, recommend products based on past purchases, and engage customers through personalized content.

6. **Strategic Partnerships and Collaborations:**

Explore Collaborations: Seek partnerships with other businesses, influencers, or affiliates that align with your brand. Collaborative marketing efforts can expand your reach and introduce your products to new audiences.

Integration with Third-Party Apps: Integrate your Shopify store with third-party apps that enhance functionality. This could include tools for marketing automation, customer relationship management (CRM), or advanced analytics.

7. **Optimized Marketing and Advertising:**

Data-Driven Marketing: Continue leveraging data analytics for marketing decisions. Analyze customer behavior, monitor campaign performance, and iterate based on insights to maximize the effectiveness of your marketing spend.

Invest in Paid Advertising: Consider increasing investment in paid advertising channels such as Google Ads, social media advertising, and influencer marketing to boost brand visibility and attract a larger audience.

8. Enhanced Customer Support and Communication:

Scalable Customer Support Systems: Implement scalable customer support systems to handle increased inquiries and provide timely assistance. This includes chatbots, knowledge bases, and well-trained support teams.

Transparent Communication: Maintain transparent communication with customers regarding any changes, expansions, or updates to your business. Keep customers informed and engaged through various channels.

9. Optimizing for Mobile Commerce:

Mobile-Responsive Design: Ensure your Shopify store is optimized for mobile devices. With a growing number of users accessing e-commerce sites via mobile, a seamless and user-friendly mobile experience is crucial for scalability.

Mobile Payment Integration: Integrate secure and convenient mobile payment options to cater to the preferences of mobile shoppers. This includes popular mobile wallets and streamlined checkout processes.

10. Metrics for Scalability Measurement:

Performance Metrics: Continuously monitor key performance indicators (KPIs) related to scalability. These may include website traffic, conversion rates, customer acquisition costs, and revenue growth.

Customer Feedback and Satisfaction: Gauge customer satisfaction through feedback and reviews. A positive customer experience is foundational for scalability, fostering loyalty and repeat business.

11. Employee Training and Organizational Structure:

Training Programs: Invest in training programs to equip your team with the skills and knowledge needed for scaled operations. This includes training for customer support, fulfillment, and new technology implementations.

Adaptable Organizational Structure: Assess and adapt your organizational structure to support scalability. Define roles, responsibilities, and communication channels to ensure efficiency as the business grows.

12. Risk Management and Contingency Planning:

Identify Potential Risks: Conduct a thorough risk assessment to identify potential challenges associated with scaling. This may include supply chain disruptions, regulatory changes, or technological challenges.

Contingency Plans: Develop contingency plans to address identified risks. Having strategies in place to mitigate and respond to unforeseen challenges is crucial for maintaining business continuity during periods of growth.

In conclusion, scaling your e-commerce business on Shopify is a dynamic process that requires a strategic blend of technology, operations, marketing, and customer-centric approaches. By embracing these scalable strategies, businesses can navigate the challenges of growth, capitalize on new opportunities, and position themselves for sustained success in the competitive e-commerce landscape.

7.1 Strategies for Scaling Successfully

Scaling an e-commerce business successfully requires a combination of strategic planning, operational efficiency, and a customer-centric approach. In this section, we delve into key strategies that businesses can employ to navigate the complexities of scaling within the Shopify ecosystem, ensuring sustainable growth and increased profitability.

1. **Operational Streamlining:**

Automate Repetitive Tasks: Identify and automate repetitive tasks within your operations, from order processing to inventory management. Automation not only reduces the risk of errors but also frees up resources for more strategic initiatives.

Implement Scalable Systems: Invest in systems and processes that can scale seamlessly with your business. This includes order fulfillment systems, customer relationship management (CRM) tools, and robust e-commerce platforms like Shopify that can handle increased traffic and transactions.

2. **Supply Chain Optimization:**

Diversify Suppliers: Reduce dependence on a single supplier by diversifying your supply chain. This mitigates risks associated with disruptions and provides flexibility in sourcing products.

Implement Just-in-Time (JIT) Inventory: Adopt JIT inventory practices to minimize holding costs and ensure optimal stock levels. This approach allows for more agile responses to changes in demand.

3. **Technology Investment:**

Scalable Hosting Solutions: Evaluate and invest in scalable hosting solutions to accommodate increased website traffic. This ensures a smooth and responsive user experience even during peak periods.

Integration with Third-Party Apps: Leverage third-party apps that enhance functionality. Whether for marketing automation, analytics, or customer support, integrated apps can add valuable features to your Shopify store.

4. Data-Driven Marketing:

Segmented Marketing Campaigns: Utilize customer segmentation for targeted marketing campaigns. Tailor your messaging based on customer behavior, preferences, and demographics to increase the relevance of your marketing efforts.

Multichannel Marketing: Expand your marketing efforts across multiple channels. Utilize social media, email marketing, influencer collaborations, and paid advertising to reach a broader audience.

5. Customer Retention Focus:

Build Loyalty Programs: Develop and promote customer loyalty programs to incentivize repeat purchases. Reward loyal customers with exclusive discounts, early access to promotions, or special perks.

Personalized Customer Engagement: Leverage customer data to personalize your interactions. Send personalized emails, recommend products based on past purchases, and create a customized shopping experience.

6. International Expansion Strategies:

Market Research and Localization: Conduct thorough market research before expanding internationally. Understand local preferences, regulations, and cultural nuances. Localize your website content, marketing materials, and customer support for a more personalized experience.

Optimized Logistics and Shipping: Optimize logistics and shipping processes to cater to international customers. Provide transparent shipping costs, options, and delivery times to enhance the overall customer experience.

7. Strategic Partnerships and Collaborations:

Strategic Alliances: Forge strategic partnerships with other businesses or influencers in your industry. Collaborate on marketing campaigns, joint ventures, or co-branded products to tap into new audiences.

Affiliate Marketing Programs: Implement affiliate marketing programs to leverage the reach of influencers or affiliates. This can drive traffic and sales through partnerships with individuals or organizations promoting your products.

8. Mobile-First Approach:

Mobile-Optimized Design: Prioritize a mobile-first approach in your website design. Ensure that your Shopify store is optimized for a seamless and user-friendly experience on mobile devices.

Mobile Payment Integration: Integrate popular mobile payment options to cater to the preferences of mobile shoppers. Simplify the checkout process for mobile users.

9. Employee Training and Development:

Continuous Training Programs: Invest in continuous training programs for your employees. Equip them with the skills needed to adapt to changing roles and responsibilities as the business scales.

Cross-Functional Collaboration: Foster a culture of collaboration and cross-functional communication. Break down silos within the organization to enhance efficiency and agility.

10. Metrics Monitoring and Analysis:

Key Performance Indicators (KPIs): Continuously monitor key performance indicators relevant to scalability. This includes metrics like website traffic, conversion rates, customer acquisition costs, and revenue growth.

Iterative Analysis: Conduct iterative analysis of data to identify trends, patterns, and areas for improvement. Regularly reassess strategies based on data insights to drive continuous optimization.

11. Customer Feedback Utilization:

Feedback Loops: Establish feedback loops to gather insights from customers. Act on both positive and negative feedback to enhance products, services, and overall customer satisfaction.

Surveys and Reviews: Implement surveys and encourage customers to leave reviews. Use this information to gauge customer sentiment and identify opportunities for improvement.

12. Agile Risk Management:

Risk Assessment: Conduct regular risk assessments to identify potential challenges associated with scaling. Anticipate risks related to supply chain, market shifts, or technological changes.

Agile Contingency Plans: Develop agile contingency plans to respond to unforeseen challenges. A proactive and adaptable approach to risk management is essential for maintaining business continuity.

In conclusion, successfully scaling your e-commerce business within the Shopify framework requires a holistic approach that combines operational excellence, technology utilization, and a deep understanding of customer dynamics. By adopting these strategic strategies, businesses can navigate the complexities of scaling, capitalize on new opportunities, and set the stage for sustained growth in the competitive e-commerce landscape.

7.2 Handling Increased Traffic and Orders

As your e-commerce business scales, handling increased traffic and managing a surge in orders becomes paramount to ensure a seamless customer experience. In this section, we explore strategies and best practices within the Shopify ecosystem to efficiently handle heightened website traffic and a surge in order volumes.

1. **Scalable Hosting Solutions:**

Evaluate Hosting Providers: Regularly assess your hosting provider's capabilities to handle increased traffic. Consider shifting to scalable hosting solutions that can dynamically adapt to fluctuations in demand.

Content Delivery Networks (CDNs): Implement CDNs to distribute website content across servers globally. This reduces latency, enhances load times, and ensures a consistent user experience regardless of geographic location.

2. **Optimize Website Performance:**

Image Compression: Compress and optimize images to reduce page load times. Large image files can contribute to slow website performance, especially during peak traffic periods.

Minimize HTTP Requests: Streamline your website by minimizing the number of HTTP requests. Combine CSS and JavaScript files, and use browser caching to reduce server load.

3. **Enhanced Server Configuration:**

Upgrade Server Specifications: Assess your server's specifications and upgrade if necessary to handle increased traffic. This may involve increasing processing power, memory, or storage capacity.

Load Balancing: Implement load balancing to evenly distribute traffic across multiple servers. This ensures optimal performance and prevents any single server from becoming a bottleneck.

4. **Caching Mechanisms:**

Browser Caching: Leverage browser caching to store static files on visitors' devices. This reduces the need for repeated downloads and accelerates page loading times for returning customers.

Full-Page Caching: Implement full-page caching to generate and store complete page content. This significantly reduces the server load during periods of high traffic.

5. **Efficient Checkout Process:**

Streamlined Checkout: Optimize the checkout process for efficiency. Implement a single-page or minimal-step checkout to reduce friction and decrease the likelihood of abandoned carts.

Guest Checkout Option: Offer a guest checkout option to streamline the purchase process for first-time customers. Simplify account creation or allow customers to proceed without creating an account.

6. Inventory and Order Management Systems:

Real-Time Inventory Updates: Integrate systems that provide real-time updates on inventory levels. This ensures accurate product availability information on your website and minimizes the risk of overselling.

Order Processing Automation: Implement automation for order processing, including invoice generation, label printing, and tracking updates. This reduces manual workload during peak order periods.

7. Customer Communication:

Clear Shipping Information: Communicate shipping information, including estimated delivery times and any potential delays. Transparent communication helps manage customer expectations.

Proactive Customer Updates: Proactively update customers on the status of their orders. Automated order status emails and tracking information enhance customer confidence and reduce inquiries.

8. Scalable Payment Processing:

Payment Gateway Assessment: Ensure your chosen payment gateway can handle increased transaction volumes. Evaluate the scalability of your payment processing system and consider alternative gateways if needed.

Multiple Payment Options: Offer a variety of payment options to cater to diverse customer preferences. This includes credit cards, digital wallets, and other popular payment methods.

9. Customer Support Readiness:

Scalable Customer Support Systems: Prepare your customer support team for increased inquiries. Implement scalable customer support systems, including chatbots, FAQs, and efficient ticketing systems.

Extended Support Hours: Consider extending customer support hours during peak periods to address inquiries promptly. Provide clear channels for customers to reach support, such as live chat, email, or phone.

10. Monitoring and Analytics:

Real-Time Monitoring: Utilize real-time monitoring tools to track website performance, server health, and traffic patterns. This enables proactive identification and resolution of potential issues.

Analytics for Insights: Leverage analytics tools to gain insights into customer behavior during peak times. Analyze data to identify popular products, pages, and trends to inform future scalability strategies.

11. Preventive Load Testing:

Load Testing: Conduct regular load testing on your website to simulate high-traffic scenarios. Identify potential bottlenecks and address them proactively to ensure a smooth experience during actual peak periods.

Capacity Planning: Based on load testing results, engage in capacity planning to determine the optimal resources needed to handle increased traffic and orders.

12. Contingency Planning:

Emergency Response Plan: Develop an emergency response plan to address unforeseen issues promptly. Outline procedures for handling server crashes, payment gateway failures, or other critical incidents.

Communication Protocols: Establish communication protocols for informing customers about any disruptions and the steps being taken to resolve issues. Transparent communication builds trust during challenging situations.

In summary, handling increased traffic and orders as your e-commerce business scales requires a combination of technological readiness, operational efficiency, and customer-centric approaches. By implementing these strategies within the Shopify ecosystem, businesses can ensure a resilient and high-performance online shopping experience, even during periods of heightened demand.

7.3 Expanding Your Product Line and Market Reach

As your e-commerce business matures, the strategic expansion of both your product line and market reach becomes instrumental in sustaining growth. In this section, we explore effective strategies within the Shopify ecosystem to successfully diversify your product offerings and broaden your market presence.

1. **Market Research and Trend Analysis:**

Identify Emerging Trends: Conduct thorough market research to identify emerging trends within your industry. Stay attuned to evolving consumer preferences, technological advancements, and market shifts that may present new opportunities.

Competitor Analysis: Analyze competitors to understand gaps in the market or areas where you can differentiate your product offerings. Identify successful products and assess the potential for similar or complementary offerings in your catalog.

2. **Diversification Strategies:**

Complementary Products: Introduce products that complement your existing offerings. This encourages customers to make multiple purchases, increasing the average order value.

Seasonal or Limited Edition Releases: Consider launching seasonal or limited edition products to create excitement and urgency among your customer base. This strategy can drive sales spikes during specific periods.

3. Supplier and Production Partnerships:

Forge Strategic Partnerships: Build strong relationships with suppliers and manufacturers. Consider exclusive partnerships that provide you access to unique or customized products, giving your store a competitive edge.

Quality Control: Maintain strict quality control standards to ensure consistency across your product line. Reliable suppliers contribute to customer trust and satisfaction.

4. International Expansion:

Evaluate Global Opportunities: Explore opportunities for international expansion. Assess the demand for your products in different regions and adapt your marketing and logistics strategies accordingly.

Localized Marketing: Tailor marketing efforts to resonate with local audiences. Consider translating product descriptions, adapting promotional campaigns, and addressing regional preferences.

5. Multichannel Selling:

Explore Additional Sales Channels: Expand beyond your Shopify store by exploring additional sales channels. Consider integrating with popular marketplaces, social media platforms, or even brick-and-mortar retailers.

Sync Inventory and Orders: Implement systems that sync inventory and orders seamlessly across multiple channels. This ensures accurate stock levels and prevents overselling.

6. **E-commerce Collaborations:**

Collaborate with Other E-commerce Brands: Partner with complementary e-commerce brands for joint ventures or collaborative product launches. This can expose your products to new audiences and create synergies between brands.

Affiliate Marketing: Implement affiliate marketing programs to leverage influencers or affiliates who can promote your products to their followers.

7. **Product Bundling and Upselling:**

Create Attractive Bundles: Package related products into attractive bundles. This encourages customers to purchase multiple items together, often at a discounted price, boosting overall sales.

Implement Upselling Strategies: Implement upselling techniques by suggesting higher-end or upgraded products during the purchasing process. This maximizes the value of each transaction.

8. Customer Feedback Utilization:

Gather Customer Insights: Utilize customer feedback to understand their needs, preferences, and desires. Conduct surveys, read product reviews, and engage with customers on social media to gather valuable insights.

Incorporate Customer Suggestions: Act on customer suggestions by incorporating popular requests into your product development strategy. This not only enhances your product line but also fosters a sense of customer involvement.

9. Content Marketing and Storytelling:

Highlight Unique Product Stories: Develop compelling product narratives that highlight the uniqueness of each item. Use storytelling in your product descriptions, blog posts, and social media content to create an emotional connection with customers.

Educational Content: Create educational content around your products. This could include tutorials, how-to guides, or lifestyle content that showcases the benefits and versatility of your offerings.

10. Optimized SEO Strategies:

Keyword Research: Conduct thorough keyword research to identify terms related to your expanded product line. Optimize product listings, category pages, and content to improve visibility in search engine results.

Content Diversity: Diversify your website content to encompass a broader range of products. This includes creating category-specific content, blog posts, and landing pages to capture a wider audience.

11. Social Media Engagement:

Visual Storytelling: Leverage visual storytelling on social media platforms to showcase your expanded product line. Use images, videos, and user-generated content to engage your audience and generate excitement around new offerings.

Interactive Campaigns: Run interactive campaigns, polls, or contests to involve your audience in product selection or naming. This not only builds anticipation but also encourages participation.

12. Data-Driven Decision-Making:

Analytics Utilization: Utilize analytics tools to track the performance of your expanded product line. Monitor sales data, customer behavior, and conversion rates to gain insights and make data-driven decisions.

Iterative Optimization: Continuously iterate and optimize your product offerings based on performance metrics. Retire underperforming products and invest resources in those that resonate well with your audience.

In conclusion, successfully expanding your product line and market reach within the Shopify ecosystem involves a strategic blend of market insights, diversified offerings, and effective marketing strategies. By adopting these proven strategies, businesses can position themselves for sustained growth, capture new market segments, and solidify their presence in the competitive e-commerce landscape.

Chapter 8: Troubleshooting Common Challenges

Navigating the e-commerce landscape, even within the robust framework of Shopify, is not without its challenges. In this chapter, we address common hurdles that e-commerce entrepreneurs may encounter and provide practical solutions to troubleshoot these issues effectively. From technical glitches to customer service concerns, this guide equips you with the knowledge to overcome obstacles and maintain a resilient and successful Shopify store.

1. **Technical Glitches and Website Downtime:**

Regular Performance Checks: Conduct regular performance checks on your website to identify potential technical issues. Utilize tools and services to monitor website uptime and respond promptly to any disruptions.

Backup Systems: Implement backup systems to ensure data integrity and facilitate a quick recovery in the event of a technical glitch. Regularly test backup and recovery processes to guarantee their effectiveness.

2. Cart Abandonment:

Streamlined Checkout Process: Optimize the checkout process for simplicity and efficiency. Minimize the number of steps required to complete a purchase to reduce the likelihood of cart abandonment.

Retargeting Campaigns: Implement retargeting campaigns through email or ads to remind customers of their abandoned carts. Offer incentives such as discounts or free shipping to encourage completion of the purchase.

3. Inventory Management Challenges:

Real-Time Inventory Tracking: Utilize inventory management tools that offer real-time tracking. This prevents overselling, minimizes the risk of stockouts, and enhances overall inventory accuracy.

Automated Restocking Alerts: Set up automated alerts for low-stock items. This allows you to reorder products promptly and maintain a consistent supply chain.

4. Customer Service Bottlenecks:

Multichannel Support: Offer customer support through multiple channels, including live chat, email, and phone. Distribute customer inquiries effectively to prevent bottlenecks and ensure timely responses.

Knowledge Base: Create a comprehensive knowledge base or FAQs section to address common customer queries. Empower customers to find answers independently, reducing the burden on customer support.

5. **Payment Processing Issues:**

Diverse Payment Options: Provide customers with diverse payment options to accommodate various preferences. Regularly test payment processing functionality to identify and resolve any issues promptly.

Clear Communication: Communicate clearly with customers about payment processes and potential issues. Promptly address any payment-related concerns raised by customers to maintain trust.

6. **Shipping Challenges:**

Transparent Shipping Information: Communicate shipping information, including costs and delivery times, during the checkout process. Transparency builds customer trust and helps manage expectations.

Diverse Shipping Partners: Collaborate with multiple shipping partners to offer varied delivery options. Evaluate and choose reliable carriers to minimize shipping delays and issues.

7. **Security Concerns:**

SSL Certificates: Ensure your website is secured with SSL certificates to encrypt data transmission and provide a secure environment for customer transactions. Display trust badges to reassure customers about the security of their information.

Regular Security Audits: Conduct regular security audits to identify vulnerabilities. Implement security measures such as two-factor authentication and robust password policies to protect customer accounts and sensitive data.

8. **Conversion Rate Optimization (CRO):**

A/B Testing: Implement A/B testing on various elements of your website, including product pages, CTAs, and checkout processes. Analyze the performance of different variants to identify and implement optimizations.

User Feedback Integration: Gather user feedback to understand pain points and areas for improvement. Integrate customer suggestions into your CRO strategy for an enhanced user experience.

9. **Compliance and Legal Issues:**

Stay Informed on Regulations: Stay informed about e-commerce regulations and consumer protection laws. Regularly review and update your store policies to ensure compliance with legal requirements.

Secure Customer Data: Prioritize the security and privacy of customer data. Implement measures such as GDPR compliance and transparent data handling practices to build trust with your customer base.

10. Adapting to Market Trends:

Continuous Market Research: Stay ahead of market trends by conducting continuous market research. Regularly assess customer preferences, emerging technologies, and industry shifts to adapt your product offerings and marketing strategies.

Agile Business Strategies: Foster an agile mindset within your business. Be prepared to pivot strategies based on evolving market conditions, ensuring your store remains relevant and competitive.

11. Crisis Management:

Preparedness Plan: Develop a crisis management plan that outlines steps to be taken in case of unexpected events. This could include disruptions in supply chains, economic downturns, or global crises. Having a plan in place ensures a more organized response during challenging times.

Transparent Communication: Communicate transparently with customers during crises. Keep them informed about any disruptions to operations, shipping delays, or changes in business practices. Transparency fosters understanding and trust.

12. Adapting to Platform Updates:

Stay Informed: Stay informed about updates and changes to the Shopify platform. Regularly check for announcements, release notes, and new features. Ensure your store is compatible with the latest updates to benefit from enhanced functionality and security.

Testing Environment: Before implementing major updates, test them in a controlled environment to identify any potential conflicts with your existing setup. This proactive approach minimizes the risk of disruptions when changes are applied.

In conclusion, troubleshooting common challenges in the e-commerce landscape requires a proactive and adaptive approach. By addressing these issues systematically, businesses can enhance their operational resilience, provide a positive customer experience, and position themselves for sustained success within the Shopify ecosystem.

8.1 Overcoming Sales Plateaus

Experiencing a sales plateau can be a perplexing challenge for e-commerce entrepreneurs. When your once-booming sales seem to reach a stagnant phase, it's crucial to strategize and break through this barrier. In this section, we explore effective ways to overcome sales plateaus within the Shopify framework and revitalize your online business.

1. **Performance Analysis:**

Review Historical Data: Analyze historical sales data to identify patterns and potential causes for the plateau. Look for correlations with external factors, seasonal trends, or changes in consumer behavior that may influence sales.

Product Performance Assessment: Evaluate the performance of individual products. Identify top-selling items and those experiencing a decline in popularity. This insight helps in adjusting your product mix for better results.

2. **Customer Feedback and Surveys:**

Gather Customer Insights: Reach out to your customer base for feedback on their shopping experience. Use surveys or direct communication to understand their preferences, concerns, and expectations.

Identify Pain Points: Identify any pain points customers may be experiencing, such as issues with the checkout process, dissatisfaction with product variety, or concerns about shipping costs.

3. **Marketing Strategy Revitalization:**

Assess Marketing Channels: Evaluate the performance of your current marketing channels. Identify which channels are driving the most traffic and conversions and reallocate resources accordingly.

Explore New Marketing Avenues: Explore new marketing avenues or experiment with different strategies. This could include influencer marketing, content marketing, or collaborations to reach untapped audiences.

4. Product Bundling and Promotions:

Create Attractive Bundles: Introduce product bundles or exclusive promotions to incentivize larger purchases. Bundling complementary items at a discounted price encourages customers to increase their order value.

Limited-Time Offers: Implement limited-time offers or flash sales to create a sense of urgency. This tactic can stimulate immediate purchases and inject new energy into your sales.

5. Customer Loyalty Programs:

Implement Loyalty Programs: Launch a customer loyalty program to reward repeat purchasers. Offer points, discounts, or exclusive perks to incentivize customers to choose your store for their ongoing needs.

Engage with Loyal Customers: Engage with your existing loyal customer base. Solicit their opinions, involve them in exclusive promotions, and make them feel appreciated.

6. Product and Store Refresh:

Update Product Catalog: Refresh your product catalog by introducing new items or variants. Stay attuned to market trends and customer demands to ensure your offerings remain appealing and competitive.

Revamp Store Design: Consider updating your store's design for a fresh look. A visually appealing and user-friendly interface can re-ignite interest and attract both new and returning customers.

7. Customer Retargeting Strategies:

Utilize Retargeting Ads: Implement retargeting ad campaigns to reach customers who have previously visited your site. Remind them of products they viewed or abandoned in their carts to encourage them to complete the purchase.

Email Marketing Sequences: Develop targeted email sequences for different customer segments. Use personalized messages, exclusive offers, and dynamic content to re-engage customers and prompt them to return to your store.

8. Collaborations and Partnerships:

Explore Collaborations: Seek collaborations with other businesses or influencers in your industry. Partnering for joint promotions or exclusive products can expand your reach and introduce your brand to new audiences.

Affiliate Marketing Programs: Establish affiliate marketing programs to leverage partners who can drive traffic and sales to your store. Offer attractive commissions to incentivize affiliates.

9. Optimized Customer Experience:

Enhance User Interface: Optimize your website's user interface to ensure a seamless and enjoyable shopping experience. A user-friendly design, intuitive navigation, and clear calls to action can positively impact conversion rates.

Responsive Customer Support: Provide responsive and helpful customer support. Address queries promptly, resolve issues efficiently, and ensure that customer's feel valued and supported throughout their shopping journey.

10. Strategic Pricing Adjustments:

Competitive Pricing Analysis: Conduct a competitive pricing analysis to ensure your products are competitively priced in the market. Adjust prices strategically based on perceived value, discounts, or promotions.

Implement Dynamic Pricing: Consider implementing dynamic pricing strategies, where prices are adjusted based on market demand, competitor pricing, or other relevant factors.

11. Social Media Engagement:

Boost Social Media Presence: Strengthen your social media presence by consistently posting engaging content. Use social platforms to connect with your audience, showcase products, and participate in relevant conversations.

Interactive Campaigns: Run interactive campaigns or contests on social media to encourage user participation. User-generated content and community engagement can boost brand visibility.

12. Continuous Data Analysis:

Utilize Analytics Tools: Leverage analytics tools to continuously monitor and analyze website and sales performance. Identify trends, track customer behavior, and use data-driven insights to inform strategic decisions.

Iterative Optimization: Adopt an iterative optimization approach. Regularly revisit and refine your strategies based on performance metrics, ensuring a dynamic and adaptive approach to your e-commerce operations.

In conclusion, overcoming sales plateaus in the Shopify ecosystem requires a multifaceted approach that addresses various aspects of your business. By combining data analysis, customer engagement strategies, and continuous optimization, you can revitalize your online store, attract new customers, and reignite growth in a competitive e-commerce landscape.

8.2 Dealing with Customer Service Issues

Exceptional customer service is the cornerstone of a successful e-commerce business. However, dealing with customer service issues is an inevitable part of managing an online store. In this section, we explore effective strategies within the Shopify framework to address and resolve customer service issues, ensuring customer satisfaction and loyalty.

1. **Prompt Communication:**

Timely Responses: Prioritize timely responses to customer inquiries. Acknowledge their concerns promptly, even if a comprehensive solution requires more time. Swift communication demonstrates attentiveness and care.

2. **Empathetic Approach:**

Understanding Customer Concerns: Approach customer interactions with empathy. Understand their concerns, acknowledge any inconvenience they may have experienced, and express a genuine commitment to resolving the issue.

3. **Clear Communication:**

Transparent Communication: Provide clear and transparent communication regarding the issue at hand. Clearly explain the steps you are taking to address the problem, the expected resolution timeline, and any necessary actions from the customer.

4. **Problem Resolution Process:**

Effective Troubleshooting: Implement an efficient problem-resolution process. Train customer service representatives to troubleshoot common issues effectively and provide step-by-step guidance to customers.

Escalation Protocols: Establish escalation protocols for complex issues. Ensure that frontline support can escalate cases to more experienced staff or relevant departments when necessary.

5. **Comprehensive FAQs and Knowledge Base:**

Detailed FAQs: Develop a comprehensive FAQ section and knowledge base on your website. Anticipate common customer queries and provide detailed answers. Encourage customers to check these resources before reaching out for support.

6. **Customer Feedback Utilization:**

Feedback Analysis: Analyze customer feedback to identify recurring issues. Use this information to address root causes and implement preventive measures. Actively seek feedback and leverage it as a valuable tool for continuous improvement.

7. **Effective Training Programs:**

Continuous Training: Invest in ongoing training programs for customer service representatives. Ensure they are well-versed in product knowledge, problem-solving techniques, and effective communication skills.

Handling Difficult Situations: Equip staff with strategies for handling difficult situations. This includes dealing with irate customers, resolving disputes, and maintaining professionalism under challenging circumstances.

8. **Automated Support Systems:**

Chatbots and Automated Responses: Implement chatbots or automated responses to handle routine queries efficiently. These systems can provide quick answers to common questions, freeing up human support agents for more complex issues.

9. **Proactive Communication:**

Proactive Issue Alerts: Implement systems that proactively alert customers about any known issues or delays. Being transparent about potential challenges demonstrates a commitment to customer satisfaction and manages expectations.

10. **Personalized Customer Interactions:**

Personalized Support: Strive for personalized customer interactions. Use customer data to address them by name and reference their order history. Personalization creates a positive customer experience and fosters a sense of importance.

11. **Quality Assurance Checks:**

Regular Quality Assurance: Conduct regular quality assurance checks on customer service interactions. Monitor recorded calls, review email correspondence, and assess chat transcripts to ensure consistency and adherence to service standards.

12. **Post-Resolution Follow-Up:**

Follow-Up Communications: After resolving an issue, follow up with customers to ensure their satisfaction. Seek feedback on the resolution process and inquire if there are additional ways you can enhance their experience.

13. Social Media Monitoring:

Active Social Media Presence: Maintain an active presence on social media platforms. Monitor comments, messages, and mentions to address customer concerns promptly. Responding publicly demonstrates your commitment to customer care.

14. Customer Compensation Strategies:

Appropriate Compensation: When appropriate, offer compensation for inconveniences. This could include discounts, freebies, or expedited shipping. Thoughtful compensation can turn a negative experience into a positive one.

15. Data Security and Privacy:

Prioritize Data Security: Ensure the security and privacy of customer data. Implement robust cybersecurity measures to protect sensitive information. Communicate your commitment to data security to build customer trust.

16. Continuous Improvement Culture:

Feedback Integration: Integrate customer feedback into a continuous improvement culture. Regularly review customer service processes, identify areas for enhancement, and implement changes to raise service quality.

In conclusion, effectively dealing with customer service issues within the Shopify ecosystem requires a proactive and customer-centric approach. By prioritizing communication, training, and continuous improvement, businesses can not only resolve issues efficiently but also build lasting relationships with their customers, fostering trust and loyalty.

8.3 Staying Competitive in the E-commerce Landscape

In the dynamic and competitive e-commerce landscape, staying ahead of the curve is essential for sustained success. This section explores strategies within the Shopify framework to ensure your online store remains competitive, attracting and retaining customers in a rapidly evolving market.

1. **Market Research and Trend Analysis:**

Continuous Research: Stay abreast of market trends and consumer behavior through continuous research. Regularly analyze industry reports, competitor strategies, and emerging technologies to identify opportunities and potential areas for improvement.

2. **Competitor Analysis:**

Thorough Competitor Assessment: Conduct a thorough analysis of your competitors. Identify their strengths, weaknesses, and unique selling propositions. Use this information to differentiate your brand and capitalize on areas where you can excel.

3. **Agile Business Strategies:**

Adaptability: Foster an agile mindset within your business. Be prepared to adapt strategies based on changing market conditions, consumer preferences, and technological advancements. Agility allows you to pivot quickly in response to evolving trends.

4. **Diversified Product Offerings:**

Expanded Product Catalog: Continuously assess and expand your product catalog. Introduce new items, variations, or complementary products to cater to diverse customer needs. A diverse product offering can attract a broader audience.

5. **Enhanced Customer Experience:**

Seamless User Experience: Prioritize a seamless and enjoyable user experience on your website. Optimize navigation, ensure fast loading times, and implement intuitive design elements. A positive online experience encourages repeat business and referrals.

6. Innovative Marketing Strategies:

Explore New Marketing Channels: Experiment with new marketing channels to diversify your reach. Explore influencer marketing, video content, or emerging social media platforms to connect with different audience segments.

Personalized Marketing Campaigns: Implement personalized marketing campaigns based on customer behavior and preferences. Utilize data to create targeted promotions, recommendations, and personalized communications.

7. Customer Engagement and Loyalty:

Interactive Engagement: Foster interactive engagement with your audience. Utilize social media, email campaigns, and loyalty programs to keep customers engaged. Actively seek feedback and involve customers in shaping your brand.

Exclusive Loyalty Programs: Offer exclusive loyalty programs or memberships that provide added benefits to repeat customers. Loyalty initiatives build a sense of community and incentivize customers to choose your store consistently.

8. Efficient Supply Chain Management:

Streamlined Logistics: Optimize your supply chain for efficiency. Work closely with reliable suppliers, employ effective inventory management, and streamline order fulfillment processes. A well-managed supply chain contributes to faster deliveries and satisfied customers.

9. Strategic Pricing and Discounts:

Competitive Pricing: Regularly review and adjust your pricing strategy to remain competitive. Consider factors such as market demand, competitor pricing, and perceived value when setting prices.

Strategic Discounting: Implement strategic discounting during key periods such as holidays or promotional events. Consider tiered discounts or bundled promotions to encourage larger purchases.

10. Adoption of Technology:

Utilize Cutting-Edge Technology: Embrace technological advancements within the e-commerce landscape. Explore tools and features offered by Shopify, such as AR/VR integration, AI-powered recommendations, and mobile optimization, to enhance your online store's functionality.

11. Customer Reviews and Social Proof:

Leverage Positive Reviews: Actively encourage and showcase positive customer reviews. Leverage social proof to build trust and credibility. Highlight testimonials, user-generated content, and positive experiences to influence potential customers.

12. **Responsive Customer Support:**

Proactive Customer Support: Provide responsive and proactive customer support. Address inquiries promptly, resolve issues efficiently, and go the extra mile to exceed customer expectations. Exceptional customer service contributes to positive brand perception.

13. **Data-Driven Decision-Making:**

Analytical Insights: Utilize data-driven decision-making processes. Leverage analytics tools to gain insights into customer behavior, sales trends, and website performance. Data-driven strategies enable you to make informed decisions for business growth.

14. **Sustainability Initiatives:**

Environmental Responsibility: Consider incorporating sustainability initiatives into your business practices. Implement eco-friendly packaging, promote responsible sourcing, or support charitable causes. A commitment to sustainability can resonate positively with environmentally conscious consumers.

15. Adaptive SEO Strategies:

Regular SEO Audits: Conduct regular SEO audits to ensure your website remains optimized for search engines. Stay updated on search engine algorithms and adjust your SEO strategies accordingly. Effective SEO practices enhance your online visibility.

16. Cross-Channel Integration:

Multichannel Presence: Expand your reach by integrating with multiple sales channels. Utilize Shopify's capabilities to sell on various platforms, including social media, marketplaces, and brick-and-mortar locations. A diversified presence mitigates risk and reaches a broader audience.

17. Mobile Optimization:

Mobile-Friendly Design: Ensure your website is optimized for mobile devices. With a growing number of users accessing e-commerce sites via mobile, a mobile-friendly design is crucial for providing a seamless shopping experience.

In conclusion, staying competitive in the e-commerce landscape demands a combination of adaptability, innovation, and a relentless focus on customer satisfaction. By consistently reassessing and optimizing various aspects of your business within the Shopify ecosystem, you can position your online store for continued growth and success in a competitive market.

Chapter 9: Future Trends in E-commerce

As the e-commerce landscape continues to evolve, anticipating and adapting to emerging trends is paramount for sustained success. In this chapter, we explore the future trajectories and innovations shaping the e-commerce industry within the Shopify ecosystem.

1. AI-Powered Personalization:

Advanced Recommendation Engines: Artificial Intelligence (AI) will play a pivotal role in enhancing personalized shopping experiences. Advanced recommendation engines will analyze customer behavior, preferences, and purchase history to provide tailored product suggestions, increasing conversion rates and customer satisfaction.

2. Augmented Reality (AR) and Virtual Reality (VR):

Immersive Shopping Experiences: The integration of AR and VR technologies will revolutionize the online shopping experience. Customers will be able to virtually try on products, visualize furniture in their homes, or experience immersive showcases, bridging the gap between brick-and-mortar and online retail.

3. Voice Commerce:

Rise of Voice-Activated Shopping: With the growing popularity of voice-activated devices, voice commerce is set to become a prominent trend. E-commerce platforms, including Shopify, will need to optimize for voice search and provide seamless voice-activated shopping experiences for users.

4. **Sustainable and Ethical Practices:**

Eco-Friendly E-commerce: Consumers are increasingly prioritizing sustainability. E-commerce businesses will need to adopt eco-friendly practices, from sustainable packaging to environmentally conscious sourcing. Shopify will likely integrate features that enable businesses to showcase their commitment to ethical and sustainable practices.

5. **Social Commerce Integration:**

Unified Shopping and Social Platforms: The integration of social media and e-commerce will deepen. Shopify merchants will leverage social commerce features, allowing customers to browse and purchase products directly on social platforms. Seamless integration will enhance brand visibility and drive sales.

6. **Subscription-Based Models:**

Expansion of Subscription Services: E-commerce businesses will continue to embrace subscription-based models. Shopify will likely enhance tools for managing subscription services, enabling businesses to offer personalized subscription plans, manage recurring billing, and optimize customer retention strategies.

7. Blockchain for Security and Transparency:

Enhanced Security: Blockchain technology will play a vital role in bolstering security and transparency in e-commerce transactions. Shopify may integrate blockchain features to enhance payment security, traceability of products, and secure customer data.

8. Mobile-First Shopping:

Dominance of Mobile Commerce: The trend towards mobile-first shopping experiences will persist. Shopify will focus on optimizing mobile responsiveness, ensuring that online stores are seamlessly accessible and navigable on a variety of mobile devices.

9. Instant Gratification with Same-Day Delivery:

Rapid Delivery Expectations: The demand for expedited shipping and same-day delivery will rise. E-commerce platforms, including Shopify, will need to facilitate integrations with local delivery services to meet consumer expectations for instant gratification.

10. Integration of Social and Environmental Impact Metrics:

Transparent Reporting: Shopify may introduce features that allow businesses to transparently report on their social and environmental impact. Metrics such as carbon footprint, fair labor practices, and community contributions will become important considerations for consumers.

11. Dynamic and Interactive Content:

Engaging Content Formats: The future of e-commerce will involve dynamic and interactive content formats. Shopify merchants will leverage interactive product displays, shoppable videos, and immersive storytelling to captivate and engage customers.

12. Inclusive and Diverse Branding:

Celebration of Diversity: Inclusivity and diversity will be integral to brand messaging. Shopify businesses will align their branding with diverse and inclusive values, ensuring representation in product offerings, marketing campaigns, and overall brand identity.

13. Cryptocurrency Payments:

Mainstream Cryptocurrency Transactions: Cryptocurrency acceptance will likely become more mainstream. Shopify may incorporate additional cryptocurrency payment options, allowing businesses to cater to a growing segment of consumers who prefer digital currencies.

14. AI-Driven Customer Service:

Enhanced Chatbots and Virtual Assistants: The role of AI in customer service will expand. Advanced chatbots and virtual assistants powered by AI will provide instant and personalized support, handling routine queries and elevating the overall customer service experience.

15. Biometric Security Measures:

Biometric Authentication: Enhanced security measures will include biometric authentication for account access and transactions. Shopify may integrate biometric features, such as fingerprint or facial recognition, to ensure secure and convenient transactions.

16. Dynamic Pricing Optimization:

Algorithmic Pricing Strategies: Dynamic pricing optimization algorithms will evolve. Shopify merchants will leverage sophisticated pricing strategies that dynamically adjust based on real-time market conditions, competitor pricing, and customer behavior.

17. Innovations in AR Advertising:

AR-Powered Advertising Campaigns: AR will extend to advertising, allowing businesses to create interactive and immersive ad campaigns. Shopify may introduce tools for businesses to seamlessly integrate AR elements into their online advertising strategies.

As we venture into the future of e-commerce, Shopify's role in facilitating these innovations will be pivotal. By staying attuned to these emerging trends and proactively adapting to the evolving landscape, businesses within the Shopify ecosystem can position themselves for sustained growth and success.

9.1 Exploring Emerging Technologies

The e-commerce landscape is undergoing a transformative journey fueled by the integration of cutting-edge technologies. In this section, we delve into the exploration of emerging technologies that are reshaping the future of online retail within the Shopify ecosystem.

1. **Artificial Intelligence (AI):**

Dynamic Personalization: AI is revolutionizing customer experiences through dynamic personalization. Within the Shopify framework, AI-driven algorithms analyze user behavior, preferences, and purchase history to provide tailored product recommendations. This level of personalization enhances engagement and boosts conversion rates.

2. Augmented Reality (AR) and Virtual Reality (VR):

Immersive Shopping Experiences: AR and VR technologies are creating immersive shopping experiences. Shopify merchants are leveraging AR to allow customers to virtually try on products or visualize items in their real-world environment. VR is being explored for virtual storefronts, enhancing the online shopping journey.

3. Voice Commerce:

Conversational Shopping: Voice commerce is emerging as a convenient way for customers to interact with e-commerce platforms. In the Shopify ecosystem, businesses are exploring voice-activated shopping experiences, where users can browse products, add items to their cart, and complete transactions using voice commands.

4. Blockchain Technology:

Enhanced Security and Transparency: Blockchain is gaining prominence for its role in enhancing security and transparency. Within Shopify, blockchain may be integrated to secure transactions, protect customer data, and provide a transparent supply chain. This technology ensures a tamper-resistant and trustworthy e-commerce environment.

5. **Progressive Web Apps (PWAs):**

Optimized Mobile Experiences: PWAs are revolutionizing mobile experiences within the Shopify ecosystem. These apps offer faster loading times, offline functionality, and seamless navigation, providing users with a native app-like experience on mobile devices. Shopify businesses are adopting PWAs to enhance mobile optimization.

6. **5G Technology:**

High-Speed Connectivity: The advent of 5G technology is shaping the future of e-commerce by providing high-speed connectivity. In the Shopify environment, businesses can leverage 5G for faster website loading, seamless video content, and enhanced mobile experiences, ensuring a smoother online shopping journey.

7. **Biometric Authentication:**

Secure and Seamless Transactions: Biometric authentication is evolving to secure transactions within the Shopify framework. Fingerprints, facial recognition, or other biometric data may be employed to enhance account security and streamline the checkout process, providing a secure and convenient user experience.

8. **Machine Learning for Dynamic Pricing:**

Algorithmic Pricing Strategies: Machine learning is driving dynamic pricing strategies. Shopify businesses can utilize machine learning algorithms to analyze market conditions, competitor pricing, and customer behavior. This enables the implementation of dynamic pricing models that optimize product prices in real time.

9. **Extended Reality (XR):**

Integration of AR and VR: Extended Reality (XR) encompasses both AR and VR technologies. Within Shopify, XR can be employed to create interactive and immersive shopping environments. XR-powered features may include virtual try-ons, 360-degree product views, and engaging AR advertising campaigns.

10. **Edge Computing:**

Faster Processing and Reduced Latency: Edge computing is enhancing the speed and efficiency of e-commerce operations. In the Shopify ecosystem, edge computing may be utilized to process data closer to the user, reducing latency and improving the overall performance of online stores, especially during peak traffic periods.

11. **Natural Language Processing (NLP):**

Conversational Commerce: Natural Language Processing (NLP) is driving conversational commerce within Shopify. Businesses can implement chatbots and virtual assistants that understand and respond to customer inquiries in natural language. This technology streamlines customer interactions and provides instant support.

12. Smart Logistics and Delivery:

Optimized Supply Chain: Emerging technologies are reshaping logistics and delivery processes. Shopify businesses can explore smart logistics solutions, including route optimization, real-time tracking, and automated fulfillment. These innovations contribute to faster and more efficient order deliveries.

13. Internet of Things (IoT):

Connected Shopping Experiences: The Internet of Things (IoT) is creating connected shopping experiences. Within Shopify, businesses may leverage IoT to offer smart, connected products. For example, IoT-enabled apparel with embedded sensors providing real-time fashion advice or smart home products seamlessly integrated into the e-commerce platform.

14. Cybersecurity Innovations:

Advanced Threat Detection: Cybersecurity innovations are crucial to protect e-commerce platforms. In the Shopify environment, advanced threat detection systems may be implemented to identify and thwart cyber threats, ensuring the security and privacy of customer data.

15. Quantum Computing:

Advanced Data Processing: Quantum computing holds the potential to revolutionize data processing capabilities. In the Shopify ecosystem, quantum computing may contribute to advanced analytics, providing businesses with unprecedented insights into customer behavior, market trends, and operational efficiency.

16. Responsive Design with Fluid Frameworks:

Adaptive and Fluid User Interfaces: Responsive design with fluid frameworks ensures a consistent and adaptive user interface across devices. Shopify businesses are exploring frameworks that provide a fluid and seamless experience, adapting to various screen sizes and resolutions for optimal user engagement.

17. Emphasis on Cyber-Physical Systems:

Integration of Physical and Digital Environments: Cyber-Physical Systems (CPS) integration enhances the connection between physical and digital environments. In Shopify, this could manifest as seamless synchronization between in-store inventory and online platforms, creating a unified and efficient retail ecosystem.

As we navigate the future of e-commerce within the Shopify framework, the exploration and implementation of these emerging technologies will shape the industry's trajectory. By staying proactive and adaptive, businesses can harness the power of these innovations to create a dynamic and engaging online shopping experience for their customers.

9.2 Adapting to Changing Consumer Behavior

Consumer behavior is a dynamic force that continually evolves, influenced by societal shifts, technological advancements, and global trends. In this section, we explore how businesses within the Shopify ecosystem can proactively adapt to changing consumer behavior to stay relevant and meet the evolving expectations of their target audience.

1. **Evolving Shopping Preferences:**

Multi-Channel Shopping: Consumers increasingly prefer multi-channel shopping experiences. Shopify businesses should optimize their presence across various channels, including social media, marketplaces, and physical stores if applicable. Seamless integration across channels enhances brand visibility and accessibility.

2. **Digital Engagement and Social Commerce:**

Social Media Influence: The influence of social media on purchasing decisions continues to grow. Shopify merchants should prioritize social commerce, leveraging features that enable direct purchasing through social platforms. Engaging social media content and influencer partnerships can enhance brand awareness and drive conversions.

3. **Mobile-First Approach:**

Mobile Optimization: Mobile devices are central to the modern shopping journey. Businesses on Shopify must maintain a mobile-first approach, ensuring that their websites are optimized for a seamless and user-friendly experience on smartphones and tablets.

4. **Emphasis on Sustainability:**

Ethical and Sustainable Practices: Consumers are increasingly prioritizing sustainability. Shopify businesses should integrate ethical and sustainable practices into their operations, from eco-friendly packaging to transparent sourcing. Highlighting these efforts can resonate positively with environmentally conscious consumers.

5. **Demand for Personalization:**

Tailored Shopping Experiences: Personalization is a key driver of consumer satisfaction. Shopify merchants should leverage customer data to provide personalized product recommendations, targeted marketing campaigns, and customized offers. The goal is to create a unique and tailored shopping experience for each individual.

6. **Rise of Subscription-Based Models:**

Subscription Services: The popularity of subscription-based models is on the rise. Businesses on Shopify can explore and implement subscription services to offer customers convenience, exclusivity, and recurring value. This model enhances customer loyalty and provides a predictable revenue stream.

7. **Contactless and Convenient Transactions:**

Digital Payments and Contactless Transactions: The preference for contactless transactions is accelerating. Shopify businesses should prioritize digital payment options, mobile wallets, and contactless methods to enhance the convenience and safety of transactions.

8. **Real-Time Interaction and Support:**

Instant Customer Support: Consumers expect real-time interaction and support. Businesses on Shopify should invest in responsive customer support systems, including live chat, chatbots, and social media engagement, to address inquiries promptly and provide instant assistance.

9. Preference for Authentic Branding:

Authentic Brand Storytelling: Authenticity is a key factor in brand loyalty. Shopify businesses should focus on transparent and genuine brand storytelling. Highlighting the brand's values, mission, and behind-the-scenes insights can foster a deeper connection with consumers.

10. Flexibility in Fulfillment Options:

Diverse Fulfillment Choices: Consumers seek flexible fulfillment options. Businesses on Shopify can offer choices such as curbside pickup, expedited shipping, or subscription box deliveries. Providing diverse fulfillment options caters to different preferences and enhances the overall shopping experience.

11. Data Privacy Concerns:

Transparent Data Practices: Data privacy is a growing concern for consumers. Shopify businesses should prioritize transparent data practices, clearly communicating how customer data is used and protected. Implementing robust cybersecurity measures builds trust and confidence.

12. Influence of User-Generated Content:

UGC and Social Proof: User-generated content (UGC) holds significant influence. Shopify merchants can encourage customers to share their experiences through reviews, testimonials, and social media content. UGC serves as powerful social proof, influencing potential buyers.

13. Dynamic Pricing Strategies:

Strategic Pricing Adjustments: Consumer price sensitivity is a key consideration. Shopify businesses can employ dynamic pricing strategies based on market demand, competitor pricing, and customer behavior. Strategic pricing adjustments, including discounts and promotions, can impact purchasing decisions.

14. Localized and Community-Centric Approach:

Community Engagement: Localized and community-centric approaches resonate with consumers. Shopify businesses should engage with local communities, participate in events, and tailor marketing efforts to reflect regional preferences. This localized approach fosters a sense of community connection.

15. Focus on Health and Wellness:

Wellness-Related Products and Services: The emphasis on health and wellness is shaping consumer choices. Businesses on Shopify can explore offerings related to wellness, fitness, and self-care. Marketing products or services that align with health-conscious trends can capture consumer interest.

16. Continuous Digital Innovation:

Adoption of New Technologies: Consumers are drawn to digital innovation. Shopify businesses should stay abreast of emerging technologies and trends, integrating features such as augmented reality, virtual try-ons, and interactive content to create engaging and forward-looking shopping experiences.

17. Embracing Diversity and Inclusion:

Inclusive Branding: Diversity and inclusion are integral to consumer expectations. Shopify businesses should embrace inclusive branding, representing diverse demographics in marketing materials, product offerings, and overall brand identity.

Adapting to changing consumer behavior requires a proactive and customer-centric approach. Businesses within the Shopify ecosystem that stay attuned to evolving trends, prioritize customer satisfaction, and leverage the platform's innovative capabilities will be well-positioned to meet the dynamic expectations of the modern consumer.

9.3 Positioning Your Business for Long-Term Success

In the ever-evolving landscape of e-commerce, positioning your business for long-term success requires strategic planning, adaptability, and a keen understanding of market dynamics. Within the Shopify ecosystem, businesses can take proactive steps to secure their position and thrive in the competitive online marketplace.

1. **Strategic Branding and Differentiation:**

Distinctive Brand Identity: Develop a distinctive brand identity that sets your business apart. Communicate your values, mission, and unique selling propositions. In the Shopify environment, leverage customizable themes and branding tools to create a memorable and differentiated online presence.

2. **Comprehensive Market Research:**

Continuous Industry Analysis: Stay vigilant with market research to understand industry trends, consumer behaviors, and competitive landscapes. Shopify businesses can utilize analytics tools to gain insights into customer preferences, helping to refine strategies and stay ahead of market shifts.

3. Agile Business Strategies:

Flexibility and Adaptability: Foster an agile mindset within your business. Be ready to adapt strategies based on changing market conditions, technological advancements, and consumer preferences. Shopify's versatile platform allows for quick adjustments to meet evolving needs.

4. Customer-Centric Approach:

Enhanced Customer Experiences: Prioritize a customer-centric approach by consistently improving the online shopping experience. Leverage Shopify's features to provide personalized recommendations, streamline the checkout process, and gather customer feedback for continuous improvement.

5. Optimized Supply Chain Management:

Efficient Fulfillment Processes: Optimize your supply chain for efficiency. Collaborate with reliable suppliers, implement effective inventory management, and explore Shopify integrations for streamlined order fulfillment. A well-managed supply chain contributes to timely deliveries and customer satisfaction.

6. **Multi-Channel Selling:**

Diversified Sales Channels: Expand your reach through multi-channel selling. Utilize Shopify's integrations to sell on social media platforms, marketplaces, and other online channels. Diversifying sales channels mitigates risks and exposes your brand to a broader audience.

7. **Strategic Marketing Campaigns:**

Targeted Marketing Strategies: Develop targeted marketing campaigns based on customer segmentation and behavior. Utilize Shopify's marketing features to run promotions, leverage email campaigns, and implement social media advertising. Data-driven marketing enhances your brand's visibility and relevance.

8. **Data Security and Privacy Compliance:**

Robust Data Protection: Prioritize data security and privacy compliance. Implement robust cybersecurity measures to safeguard customer data. Shopify provides security features, and businesses should stay informed about data protection regulations to ensure compliance and build customer trust.

9. Continuous Innovation and Technology Adoption:

Embrace Emerging Technologies: Stay abreast of emerging technologies and innovations within the e-commerce space. Shopify regularly updates its platform with new features; businesses should explore and adopt these tools to stay technologically competitive and offer cutting-edge experiences.

10. Customer Loyalty Programs:

Engage and Retain Customers: Implement customer loyalty programs to encourage repeat business. Shopify businesses can set up loyalty tiers, offer exclusive discounts, and reward customers for their ongoing support. Building a loyal customer base contributes to long-term success.

11. Social Responsibility and Sustainability:

Ethical Business Practices: Embrace social responsibility and sustainability. Communicate your commitment to ethical practices, environmental responsibility, and community involvement. Shopify businesses can leverage these initiatives to resonate with socially conscious consumers.

12. Regular Performance Analysis:

Analytical Insights: Regularly analyze performance metrics using Shopify's analytics tools. Evaluate sales data, customer behavior, and website performance. Data-driven insights enable informed decision-making, allowing businesses to refine strategies and address areas for improvement.

13. **Adaptive SEO Strategies:**

Search Engine Optimization: Stay vigilant with SEO strategies to maintain a strong online presence. Regularly audit your website, optimize content, and stay informed about search engine algorithms. Shopify businesses can utilize SEO tools to enhance visibility and attract organic traffic.

14. **Investment in Employee Training:**

Skilled Workforce: Invest in employee training to ensure a skilled and knowledgeable workforce. A well-trained team contributes to operational efficiency, exceptional customer service, and the ability to adapt to changing demands within the Shopify ecosystem.

15. **Financial Resilience and Planning:**

Strategic Financial Management: Practice prudent financial management to ensure resilience. Plan for contingencies, monitor expenses and allocate resources strategically. Shopify businesses should leverage financial tools to track expenditures and revenues for sound financial planning.

16. Community Engagement and Brand Advocacy:

Active Community Participation: Engage with your community and foster brand advocacy. Utilize social media, participate in community events, and encourage user-generated content. Shopify businesses can leverage community engagement to build brand loyalty and enhance reputation.

17. Adaptation to Regulatory Changes:

Compliance Awareness: Stay informed about regulatory changes and compliance requirements. The e-commerce landscape is subject to evolving regulations. Shopify businesses should adapt swiftly to changes in areas such as taxation, data protection, and consumer rights.

By strategically implementing these measures within the Shopify ecosystem, businesses can position themselves for long-term success. The dynamic nature of e-commerce requires a proactive and adaptive approach, and Shopify provides a robust platform that empowers businesses to navigate challenges and seize opportunities for sustained growth.

Conclusion:

Congratulations on completing this comprehensive guide to mastering Shopify for building and maximizing your e-commerce profits. Throughout this journey, we've delved into the intricacies of establishing a successful online store, optimizing your products, perfecting your branding, implementing effective marketing strategies, and navigating the ever-evolving landscape of e-commerce.

In the vast realm of online entrepreneurship, Shopify stands as a beacon, offering a versatile and powerful platform that empowers individuals and businesses to turn their visions into reality. As we conclude this guide, let's reflect on key takeaways and the essence of achieving Shopify mastery.

1. Empowering Your E-commerce Journey:

Shopify as Your Partner: Shopify serves as more than just a platform; it's your partner in the e-commerce journey. Its user-friendly interface, customizable features, and robust tools are designed to empower entrepreneurs at every stage of their online venture.

2. Building a Strong Foundation:

Foundations of Success: A successful e-commerce business begins with a solid foundation. From setting up your Shopify store to navigating the dashboard and choosing the right plan, each step is crucial in laying the groundwork for sustained growth.

3. Product Selection and Optimization:

Key to Profitability: Your product selection and optimization strategies play a pivotal role in determining your e-commerce success. Identifying profitable niches, selecting winning products, and optimizing product pages for conversions are essential steps to drive revenue.

4. Store Design, Branding, and User Experience:

Crafting a Unique Identity: Creating a visually appealing store, building a strong brand identity, and enhancing user experience contribute to establishing a unique and memorable presence in the crowded e-commerce landscape.

5. Marketing Mastery:

Crafting Winning Campaigns: Mastering marketing strategies, including comprehensive plans, social media leverage, and effective email campaigns, is essential for reaching your target audience and driving traffic to your Shopify store.

6. Maximizing Profits:

Strategies for Growth: Pricing strategies, implementing upsells and cross-sells, and streamlining order fulfillment processes are integral components in maximizing profits. These strategies ensure that every aspect of your business contributes to the bottom line.

7. Analytics, Scaling, and Troubleshooting:

Informed Decision-Making: Utilizing Shopify analytics tools, interpreting key metrics, and making data-driven decisions are vital for understanding your business's performance. Scaling strategies and troubleshooting common challenges ensure long-term viability.

8. Adapting to Future Trends:

Staying Ahead: The e-commerce landscape is dynamic, and staying competitive requires adapting to emerging trends. Exploring technologies, understanding changing consumer behaviors, and positioning your business for the future are keys to sustained success.

9. Positioning for Long-Term Success:

Strategic Positioning: Positioning your business for long-term success involves a strategic approach. Branding, market research, agility, customer-centricity, and adaptation to emerging technologies are paramount in securing your place in the e-commerce arena.

As you embark on your Shopify mastery journey, remember that success is not a destination but a continuous process of learning, adapting, and innovating. Shopify provides the canvas, and your creativity and dedication paint the picture of your e-commerce success.

May your Shopify store thrive, your profits soar, and your entrepreneurial spirit continue to drive you toward new heights. Whether you're just starting or looking to optimize an existing business, this guide has equipped you with the knowledge and tools to navigate the exciting world of e-commerce with confidence.

Here's to your Shopify mastery and the limitless possibilities that lie ahead in your e-commerce venture. Best of luck on your journey to building and maximizing your e-commerce profits!

www.ingramcontent.com/pod-product-compliance
Lightning Source LLC
Chambersburg PA
CBHW062104220526
45471CB00010B/3598